MW00365522

PLANT-BASED
BURGERS

AND OTHER VEGAN RECIPES FOR DOGS, SUBS, WINGS AND MORE

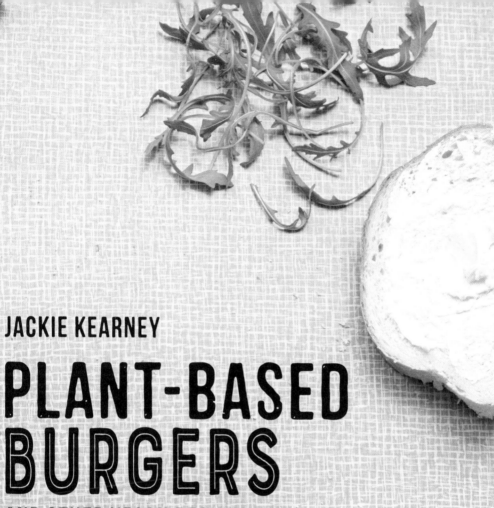

JACKIE KEARNEY

PLANT-BASED BURGERS

AND OTHER VEGAN RECIPES FOR DOGS, SUBS, WINGS AND MORE

PHOTOGRAPHY BY CLARE WINFIELD

RYLAND PETERS & SMALL
LONDON • NEW YORK

Dedication
To all the change makers.

Senior Designer Megan Smith
Design Assistance Emily Breen
Editor Miriam Catley
Production Manager Gordana Simakovic
Art Director Leslie Harrington
Editorial Director Julia Charles
Publisher Cindy Richards

Food Stylists Emily Kydd & Jackie Kearney
Props Stylists Tony Hutchinson & Alexander Breeze
Indexer Vanessa Bird

Originally published in 2018 as *Vegan Mock Meat Revolution*. This revised edition published in 2022 by Ryland Peters & Small
20–21 Jockey's Fields
London WC1R 4BW
and
341 East 116th Street
New York, NY 10029

www.rylandpeters.com

10 9 8 7 6 5 4 3 2 1

Text © Jackie Kearney 2018, 2022
Design and photographs © Ryland Peters & Small 2018, 2022

The author's moral rights have been asserted. All rights reserved. No part of this publication may be reproduced, stored in a retrieval system or transmitted in any form or by any means, electronic, mechanical, photocopying or otherwise, without the prior permission of the publisher.

ISBN 978-1-78879-421-3

A CIP record for this book is available from the Brisih Library.
US Library of Congress CIP data has been applied for.

Printed in China

Notes
• Both British (Metric) and American (Imperial plus US cups) measurements are included in these recipes for your convenience, however it is important to work with one set of measurements and not alternate between the two within a recipe.

• All spoon measurements are level unless otherwise specified.

• Ovens should be preheated to the specified temperatures. We recommend using an oven thermometer. If using a fan-assisted oven, adjust temperatures according to the manufacturer's instructions.

• When a recipe calls for the grated zest of citrus fruit, buy unwaxed fruit and wash well before using. If you can only find treated fruit, scrub well in warm soapy water before using.

MIX
Paper from responsible sources
FSC® C106563

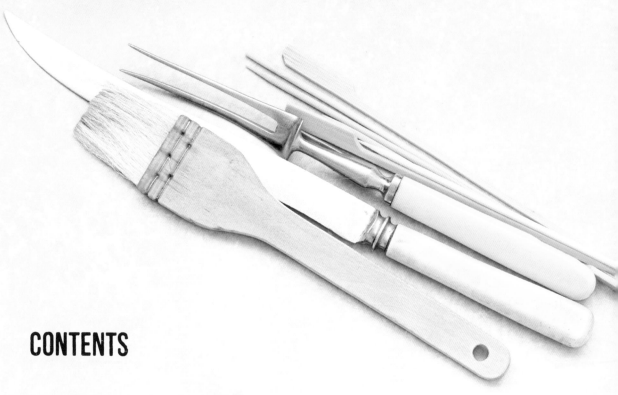

CONTENTS

INTRODUCTION 6

STORECUPBOARD INGREDIENTS 10

A FEW BASIC RECIPES 12

ASIAN STREET FOOD 16

FAUX FISH 52

FAST FOOD FAVOURITES 78

COMFORT FOOD CLASSICS 108

INDEX 142

ACKNOWLEDGMENTS 144

INTRODUCTION

It's time for a difficult discussion. I'm going to talk about meat in a vegan book.

For more than 30 years now I have heard the response, but why on earth would you want to eat meat-like food when you're a vegetarian? Omnivores would look at me in complete disbelief and confusion; if you want it, just eat it! Even fellow veggies and vegans (more veggies than vegans as there weren't so many vegans around back then) would sometimes look aghast; why would you WANT to recreate such a vile thing as flesh-like food? There appeared to be these two camps, and I fitted into neither.

As a child, I thought lamb chops with mint sauce were one of the most delicious things to eat on the planet. But as I got older, I became wholly and completely committed to not eating them simply because I didn't (and don't) want to eat sentient animals. I can understand how people may be repulsed by the idea of eating flesh, and that can lead them to become committed vegans and vegetarians. But the truth is, meat-eating doesn't repulse me. I just choose not to.

But everyone's reasons for wanting to eat more plant-based food are driven by many more complex and varied reasons other than simply not wanting to, or actually not liking it, or that eating meat or dairy makes them feel unwell. This only makes up a small proportion of plant-based eaters these days. Some describe themselves as flexitarian, pescatarian and meat-reducing. There are also diets driven by food intolerances and autoimmune responses, especially in relation to dairy and gluten. Tofu-based mock meats, such as the Vietnamese vegan 'chicken ham' and the versatile green jackfruit, make great gluten-free alternatives here. But for me, the reasons for mock meats need be no more

complicated than simply drinking alcohol-free beer or wine. For whatever reasons, sometimes people simply choose not to.

Even back in 2011, in one of the biggest moments of my cooking life, I pulled an ingredient from my own dish on MasterChef, because I believed another contestant who told me – you can't serve that rubbish (a seitan-based mock duck) to John Torode, he'll never forgive you. Believe me, it would have been the best vegan dish he'd ever eaten. My frustration at my own lack of confidence in that moment, is one of the reasons I've been so enamoured with my recent foodie trip across North America. The very thing Brits can be found criticizing them for, a sometimes bold and unapologetic attitude, was a wonderful thing when applied to food, especially vegan food. I wish I had been more bold and unapologetic with my food when I was on MasterChef – things could have turned out very differently!

But I did take that boldness forward, and I was one of the first veggie chefs to be serving green jackfruit and fried gluten (seitan) to the UK mainstream. The latter having been a kitchen staple for me since my early 20s. Back then, it was only ever the kind that came in a can and I soon learned you had to rinse the product really well in warm water to get rid of the overpowering flavour of the brine. But never one to throw the baby (or the gluten) out with the bathwater, I worked on sauces and found this to be a really adaptable product to all kinds of recipes. I remember serving a warm 'duck' salad at a party in 1994, and repeatedly responding to friends enquiries are you sure that's not really meat?'

Plant-based proteins are vital to all of our diets, but especially those of us who do not consume meat or fish, or those who want to reduce consumption

of animal-based protein. One of the great things about mock meats is the variation it provides in a more plant-based diet, for providing texture and flavour with great sources of protein. There is no doubt in my mind, plant-based alternatives will never substitute the bite of a real steak or lamb chop, or the complex flavours of seafood or bone broths – unless they are grown in a lab which is a whole other ballpark of discussion. But the idea of recreating texture and flavour without the use of animal products is far from a new one.

Some of the earliest documentation of mock meat, specifically the production of tofu as a meat substitute, can be found during the Han dynasty 206 BC–220 AD, which also coincides with some of the first recorded Buddhist scriptures and teachings being brought into China. Although Buddhism has experienced a sometimes violent history in China, it is also one of the main three religions and has shaped Chinese culture and the practice of zhai jie – the undertaking of a vegetarian fast. Buddhists practice zhai jie as a cleansing period for both mind and body, which is said to help increase our sense of compassion for everything around us. The change within ourselves is said to begin with a change in our eating habits. This vegetarian fast is often observed on Uposatha by many meat-eaters – a bit like Sabbath days in Christianity and Judaism or Ramadan in Islam, where people choose to intensify their practices and ethics. It is this wide-spread adoption of vegetarian eating, albeit on specific days, that gave rise to the proliferation of mock meat products in China.

Abstaining from eating meat for a specific period of time is also common in other countries in South East Asia, especially during the Nine Emperor Gods festival. This nine-day festival sees a proliferation of vegetarian food and is a joy to behold! My experience in Asian countries has been that products may be labelled vegetarian, but with the absence of dairy, many products are in fact vegan, it is simply that the term is far less widespread.

The social and environmental impacts of introducing more omnis to vegan meats is far greater than simply widening options for committed vegans. I want more people to enjoy more plant-based food, regardless of their other dietary choices. And I believe that embracing mock meat will help make the current rise in plant-based eating a more enduring phenomenon. I know this because I have seen hundreds of people's reactions to eating 'substitutes' for the first time – well-made and delicious mock meat substitutions – and their response is always the same. 'If I could at vegan food that tasted like this, I would choose it more often'. And for me that is what will change the fate of our little blip of existence on this planet. The maths is simple. If two billion meat-eaters halved their consumption of meat dishes for plant-based dishes, the environmental impact would be future-changing. If we used that grazing land to produce grain proteins, it would feed many more people too.

Plant-based meats and grain proteins are the future of food, and I hope the recipes in this book go some way in introducing delicious mock meat recipes into everyone's kitchen.

STORECUPBOARD INGREDIENTS

The focus of this section is to explain some of the less well-known ingredients that are useful in vegan cooking, especially in making mock meats.

TOFU/BEAN CURD Originating in early China, tofu, or bean curd, is made from soy beans. The curdled soy milk is separated into curds and a whey-like liquid. The curds are compressed into blocks of tofu, and the liquid discarded. The tofu can be prepared in a variety of ways. Silken tofu, which is very slippery and soft, is good for poaching and makes a great egg replacement in baking. Medium and firm tofu is great for marinating, baking or frying. Smoked tofu is particularly delicious and along with plain tofu can be found in supermarkets, health food shops and Chinese or other East Asian grocery stores.

BEAN CURD SHEET/SKIN This is the skin that forms during the process of making tofu. The skin is harvested and packaged either fresh or dried into sheets. These sheets are sometimes dried and twisted into sticks, which can be marinated then baked or fried. The sheets are also used to make a popular mock meat known as Vietnamese vegan 'chicken ham'.

TEMPEH Originating from Indonesia, tempeh is made from cultured soy beans. The beans are fermented and compressed into firm blocks or cakes. Tempeh retains the whole bean and is highly nutritious. It's an important source of protein in South East Asia.

VITAL WHEAT GLUTEN/SEITAN This is a key ingredient in making many popular mock meat recipes. The wheat gluten is extracted from wheat flour and can be sourced from health food stores or websites, such as Shipton Mill or Real Foods. The fine flour is mixed with herbs and spices, along with other flavours and ingredients to create a dough that is cooked to form a textured grain-based protein.

NORI This seaweed is extremely versatile and accessible. Mostly available in sheets for making sushi, they can be cut or chopped to the desired size. The seaweed can be crumbled into salt or directly into broths to add depth and flavour, especially when making faux fish recipes.

DULSE This flavoursome seaweed is my current favourite. Readily available in the UK and Europe as it grows freely around our coasts. There are also some excellent producers, such as Irish Seaweeds or Cornish Seaweed. I also use a dried seaweed sprinkle mix for flavour-enhancing and a taste of the sea.

TAPIOCA STARCH This is similar to cornflour/cornstarch, however it has a more gelatinous and sticky nature. It can be used to set puddings or thicken sauces and custards. Readily available in health food stores or online from suppliers like Real Food.

NUTRITIONAL YEAST Nutritional yeast is de-activated yeast used as a flavour enhancer. It has a rich, cheese-like and slightly nutty taste and is often added as a cheese substitute in vegan recipes. It is also rich in B vitamins. Available in health food stores and online.

LIQUID SMOKE This can be found in a variety of flavours and is readily available in shops and online. I have a preference for hickory flavour in mock meat recipes. This smoked essence or extract is highly potent and just a few drops will bring a delicious smoky flavour.

DRIED MUSHROOMS A versatile ingredient and a fantastic flavour enhancer which also brings some meaty texture to recipes. I keep a stock of mixed wild mushrooms, Chinese, shiitake and porcini. A little goes a long way. You can make your own mushroom powder by grinding any dried variety in a spice grinder, then sprinkle into stocks and sauces.

A FEW BASIC RECIPES

This section covers some basic component recipes that are used in dishes elsewhere in this book. These techniques of mock meat making can be adapted in different ways for a variety of dishes so, once you've mastered them, get creative! The recipes can be made in larger batches and frozen.

MOCK SMOKY BACON

WET MIX
2–3 tablespoons unflavoured coconut oil
1 medium onion, finely chopped
2 small sun-dried tomatoes (in olive oil), finely chopped
2 bay leaves
5 g/⅛ oz. dried dulse seaweed, soaked and finely chopped (approx. 12 g/⅓ oz. soaked weight)
100 ml/⅓ cup plus 1 tablespoon passata/strained tomatoes
110 ml/⅓ cup plus 2 tablespoons good-quality vegetable stock
2 teaspoons sea salt
1 teaspoon caraway seeds
1 teaspoon hickory liquid smoke
2 tablespoons maple syrup
2 tablespoons soy sauce

DRY MIX
250 g/9 oz. wheat gluten
2 generous tablespoons chickpea/gram flour
2 tablespoons nutritional yeast
1 teaspoon onion powder
½ teaspoon garlic powder
2 teaspoons smoked paprika
⅓ teaspoon dried sage

POACHING MIX
2 litres/2 quarts vegetable stock
150 ml/⅔ cup cider vinegar
1 tablespoon coriander seeds, lightly toasted
1 tablespoon mustard seeds, lightly toasted
4 bay leaves

MAKES 2 X 150 G/5¼ OZ. LOAVES OR 1 X 300 G/10½ OZ. LOAF

Preheat the oven to 180°C (350°F) Gas 4.

For the wet mix, in a medium frying pan/skillet, add the coconut oil and place on a medium heat. Add the onion and fry gently for 6–7 minutes until translucent. Try not to colour. Add the sun-dried tomatoes, plus any residual olive oil, and the bay leaves, and fry gently for a few minutes. Add the remaining wet mix ingredients and bring to a simmer again. Cook gently for 4–5 minutes, then discard the bay leaves. Set aside to cool.

Place the dry mix ingredients in a large bowl and add the onion mixture from the pan. Mix well and knead the dough until it comes together.

Halve the dough, then roll into a long sausage shape, approximately 5 x 7.5 cm/2 x 3 inches. Wrap the doughs in well-oiled muslin/cheesecloths, rolling and then twisting and securing each end with a little twine. Lay the wrapped doughs in a large, deep oven pan. Pour the vegetable stock into the pan and add the other poaching ingredients. Cover the pan with foil and bake in the preheated oven for 1½ hours.

Remove from the oven and poaching liquid and set aside, still wrapped, to cool. Remove the muslin/cheesecloth. Slice into rashers or dice into 'lardons'. The 'bacon' can now be fried, warmed or frozen.

AQUAFABA 'EGG'

This is simply chickpea water – the liquid from a can of chickpeas – that has taken on some of the protein from the chickpeas and forms an egg-white-like substitute. Some cooks use it to make meringue, but it's highly unstable and you have to add an excessive amount of sugar to cover the flavour of chickpeas. However, it does make an excellent ingredient in savoury food.

The best aquafaba is where the water is drained and then boiled until it is reduced by half. The reduced liquid should then be chilled, where it will become quite gelatinous.

MOCK CHKN/HOMEMADE SEITAN CHICKEN

This is a great recipe for a flavourful chicken substitute that can be made into bite-sized pieces or adapted to make escalopes, nuggets or wings.

200 g/7 oz. vital wheat gluten
2 tablespoons nutritional yeast
1 tablespoon onion powder
1 teaspoon Herbamare seasoning
½ teaspoon sea salt
½ teaspoon dried thyme
½ teaspoon dried marjoram
35 ml/2 tablespoons tahini
150 ml/⅔ cup vegetable stock

FOR THE BRAISING PAN
1–1.5 litres/1 quart–6 cups plus
    4 tablespoons vegetable stock
4 garlic cloves, slightly smashed
handful of fresh herbs, such as
    rosemary and/or thyme

flour, for dusting

MAKES APPROX. 4 ESCALOPES/20 WINGS

To prepare the mock chkn, mix together the dry ingredients in a medium bowl. In a jug/pitcher, mix together the tahini and stock. Make a well in the centre of the bowl, and pour in two thirds of the stock mixture. Combine the ingredients to make a stiff dough, adding more of the stock mixture as needed. The dough should be nice and firm. Knead well for a minute. Leave to rest for 5–10 minutes.

Preheat the oven to 170°C (325°F) Gas 4. Prepare a braising pan by adding all the ingredients into a deep oven pan and place on middle shelf in the preheated oven for 10–15 minutes.

TO MAKE CHKN 'ESCALOPES'

Place the dough on a well-floured surface and roll out to 2-cm/¾-inch thickness. To achieve an escalopedile shape, use a knife and slice the dough into 4 pieces. Roll and stretch these out to make a flattened shape. It is very springy to work with, so you may need to flatten the shapes again before baking.

TO MAKE CHKN 'WINGS'

Place the dough on a well-floured surface and roll out to 2-cm/¾-inch thickness. The shape doesn't really matter, but to achieve a wing-like shape, use a heart-shaped cookie cutter, then make a small cut into the heart shape at the top. Press the dough down on the surface to flatten and shape. It can be very springy to work with, so you may need to flatten your wing shapes again before baking.

TO MAKE CHKN 'PIECES'

Place the dough on a well-floured surface and cut into 4 pieces. Roll each piece into a large sausage shape. Once the pieces have been cooked, as instructed below, the pieces can be cooled and chopped into bite-sized pieces to use in other recipes as a substitute for chicken. These pieces can also be minced/ground using a food processor. The minced/ground chkn can then be frozen for later use.

TO COOK THE CHKN

Remove the braising pan from the oven and place the mock chkn into the pan. Cover with foil and bake in the preheated oven for 40 minutes. Remove the foil and then bake, uncovered, for a further 10–20 minutes (depending on size of the chkn pieces). Set the cooked mock chkn pieces on paper towels to drain, then serve.

VIETNAMESE VEGAN 'CHICKEN HAM'

This is a fantastic gluten-free recipe for making mock meat. The ready-made rolls are readily available in the freezer section of most Chinese or Vietnamese grocery stores, but they are also expensive and sometimes have egg added to them. This recipe uses fresh or dried bean curd sheets, which makes it very economical. The roll will freeze well after cooking too. I often make two or three rolls at the same time, and chop some into smaller pieces before freezing so I can add to stir frys, soups or make my crowd-pleasing vegan belly bits (see page 38).

1 x 200 g/7 oz. packet dried bean
    curd sheets/skins or 1 x 250 g/9 oz.
    fresh bean curd sheets/skins
¼ teaspoon bicarbonate of/baking soda
1 leek, tough dark green end removed,
    finely sliced
3 tablespoons vegetable oil
1 teaspoon salt
1 teaspoon ground white pepper
1 teaspoon white sugar (optional)
2 teaspoons mushroom powder/seasoning
1–2 fresh chillies/chiles, deseeded and
    chopped (optional)
1–2 garlic cloves, crushed (optional)

banana leaves or greaseproof paper
twine

MAKES ONE LARGE ROLL

Prepare the vegan 'chicken ham' by breaking up the bean curd sheets into a large deep pan, cover with water and add the bicarbonate of/baking soda. Stir well and bring to the boil. Simmer for 10–15 minutes until the sheets are well softened. Drain in a colander. Tip the bean curd out onto a board and finely chop. Return to the bowl one handful at a time, squeezing out any excess water.

In a frying pan/skillet, add the leek and vegetable oil. Place over a medium heat and cook for 6–7 minutes until well softened. Remove the leek from the pan and add to the bowl containing the bean curd along with the salt, pepper, sugar and mushroom powder/seasoning. You can also add other spices at this stage, such as chillies/chiles, garlic and whatever else you like.

Using a large pestle or blunt-ended rolling pin, mash the bean curd mixture to make a rough pulp.

Lay out the banana leaves or greaseproof paper, two or three pieces on top of each other, and place the mixture in the centre, making an oblong shape. Lift the longer sides and fold on top, pulling tightly like a parcel. Then fold up the ends, to make a snug fit. The roll should be approximately 12–15 cm/ 5–6 inches long and 5–7.5 cm/2–3 inches wide. If you prefer, you can make two smaller rolls, which can be easier to wrap and secure. Secure the package with twine, trimming any excess on the ends and tying like a parcel. Place the roll(s) into a steamer and cook for about 30–40 minutes.

Remove the vegan 'chicken ham' from the steamer and leave to cool, then unwrap and use as required. The 'chicken ham' can be wrapped and stored in the fridge for up to 5 days.

ASIAN
STREET FOOD

I decided to start this book with Asian street food. Despite the catch-all title, it's still the way I would describe the food that inspires me the most. Curries, dals, fried snacks, buns, skewers and big bowls of noodles. The street food of Asia is the food that lights my fire and makes me hungry at any time of day.

BUDDHA'S DELIGHT

This is one of the first recipes that introduced me to 'Buddhist meats' over 25 years ago. This bowl of soup is one of the most popular vegetarian combinations in China.

I served a version of this at one of my old supper clubs just after MasterChef in 2011, and it definitely took the diners by surprise with its meaty qualities.

The traditional full ingredients list can be exceptionally long (yes even for me!) but it's actually quite an easy dish to make. Many of the ingredients have a really long shelf life, so it's well worth a trip to the Chinese supermarket. Some red fermented bean curd has some startling additives, so check the ingredients and look for the least luminously-coloured or choose ones that use beetroot/beet juice or other natural colouring.

10 dried Chinese mushrooms
small handful of dried lily buds
small handful of dried tree ears
large pinch of dried black moss (optional)
3 tablespoons peanut or other nut/seed oil
2.5 cm/1 inch piece of fresh ginger, peeled and thinly sliced
3 garlic cloves, crushed
½ white cabbage, thinly sliced/shredded
4 long dried bean curd sticks (or 8 if using short sticks), soaked in hot water for 1 hour, then drained
200-g/7-oz. can straw mushrooms, drained and rinsed

140-g/5-oz. can bamboo shoots, drained, rinsed and sliced (larger pieces)
2 cakes of fermented red bean curd
160 g/5¾ oz. mung bean vermicelli noodles, soaked in hot water for 15 minutes, then drained
2 tablespoons vegetarian oyster/stir-fry sauce
2 teaspoons toasted sesame oil
¼ teaspoon sugar
½ teaspoon sea salt
sliced spring onion/ scallion, to garnish
soy sauce, to serve

SERVES 4

Put the dried Chinese mushrooms in a bowl and the lily buds, tree ears and black moss (if using) in another bowl. Add 250 ml/1 cup plus 1 tablespoon hot water to both bowls and soak for 15 minutes until they are soft. Drain and squeeze out the excess water, reserving the soaking water from the mushrooms.

Starting with the mushrooms, use a small paring knife to remove the stems, then lay them flat and slice thinly. Next, slice the lily buds lengthways. Trim the tree ears, removing any tough parts, and roughly chop. Drain the black moss. Set aside.

Put a tablespoon of the oil in a large wok over a medium-high heat, and fry the ginger and garlic for 30–40 seconds. Add the cabbage to the wok and fry for a few minutes until it starts to soften. Tip the contents of the wok onto a plate and return the wok to the hob/stove-top. Add the remaining oil and the mushrooms, fry for a minute or two and then add the bean curd sticks, tree ears, lily buds, straw mushrooms, black moss (if using), bamboo shoots and the reserved mushroom liquid. Add another 200 ml/generous ¾ cup of water and bring to the boil, then reduce to gentle simmer. Add the beancurd cakes and break up using the back of a spoon. Add the remaining ingredients and bring back to a simmer. Cover and leave on a low heat for 20–30 minutes. Add a further 235 ml/1 cup of water as needed. There should be enough broth to just cover everything. Serve garnished with spring onion/ scallion and soy sauce.

SPINACH DAL WITH COCONUT BACON

Bacon in dal? Really? Well, that was my response to Tim Anderson's social media post. But I trust his palate more than most, so decided to make a vegan version. And yes, the MasterChef champion is absolutely right. Bacon in dal should be an actual thing. It's the crispy and salty texture with the creamy dal that makes this dish work. There are several ways to make a vegan substitute for bacon. Soy-marinated tempeh slices are an easy one. You could use the mock smoky bacon recipe on page 12, but I'm also a fan of coconut bacon. This is a dhaba-style palak dal, similar to the kind served at roadside cafes and stops in India and Pakistan. The flavours of coconut bacon work really well alongside the spinach.

250 g/9 oz. toor dal
1 teaspoon ground turmeric
3 tablespoons vegetable oil
1 teaspoon cumin seeds
1 small red onion, finely chopped
4 large garlic cloves, crushed and then chopped
3-cm/1¼-inch piece of fresh ginger, peeled and finely chopped
2 green finger chillies/chiles, sliced lengthways
1 large tomato, finely chopped
100 g/3½ oz. spinach, roughly chopped
1–2 teaspoons sea salt, to taste
pinch of asafoetida powder
freshly squeezed juice of ½ lemon

FOR THE 'BACON'
(MAKES DOUBLE BATCH)
120 g/scant 2½ cups coconut flakes
1½ tablespoons reduced soy sauce or tamari
1 tablespoon liquid smoke (preferably Hickory)
½ tablespoon maple syrup
(*Note:* or substitute 120 g/4½ oz. ready-made coconut bacon)

baking sheet lined with baking parchment

SERVES 4–6

Preheat the oven to 170°C (325°F) Gas 3. To make the coconut bacon, scatter the coconut flakes onto the prepared baking sheet. Mix together the soy sauce or tamari, liquid smoke and maple syrup and drizzle over the coconut flakes. Mix well to coat the flakes. Place on the middle shelf in the oven and bake for about 15 minutes, turning the pieces halfway through, to get an even crispness and colour. They will crisp up a little more after cooling. Remove from the oven and leave to cool. The coconut will keep for several months in an airtight container.

Put the dal and turmeric into a heavy-based pan, add 1 litre/1 quart of water and bring to the boil. Simmer for 30 minutes over a low-medium heat, removing any scum from the top with a spoon. Remove from the heat and mash lightly. Set aside.

Put a deep frying pan/skillet over a medium heat, add the oil, then the cumin seeds. As soon as they start to splutter, add the onion and cook gently for a few minutes until softened. Add the garlic, ginger and chillies/chiles and cook for 5–6 minutes. Add the tomato, stir for 1–2 minutes and then add the spinach. Cover the pan and cook for 5–6 minutes, remove the lid and add the lentil mash along with 235 ml/1 cup of water (more if needed), the salt and asafoetida. Bring back to a simmer and cook for a further 5 minutes. Remove from the heat and finish with a squeeze of lemon. Check the seasoning before serving. Fill bowls with the dal, sprinkle coconut bacon on top and serve immediately with warm chapatis.

SWEET & SOUR MOCK 'PORK'

A classic dish on Chinese menus in the UK, this Hong Kong- or Cantonese-style recipe serves the mock meat in fried battered pieces, coated in the sticky jammy sauce. You can use the fragrant satay chicken skewers (page 41) instead of canned gluten for the mock meat in this dish or the Vietnamese vegan 'chicken ham' (see page 14) for a gluten-free alternative. I also swap out the sugar for agave syrup sometimes. This super quick recipe can be ready in 15 minutes and makes a great midweek supper.

1 tablespoon vegetable or sesame oil, plus extra for frying
2 x 280-g/10-oz. cans fried gluten mock pork, drained and rinsed
60 g/½ cup potato starch, or cornflour/cornstarch
½ teaspoon ground white pepper
2 teaspoons sea salt
4 tablespoons vegan 'egg' substitute, such as flax egg or Orgran
1 small red onion, cut into large chunks
½ red (bell) pepper, peeled, deseeded and cut into large chunks
½ green (bell) pepper, peeled, deseeded and cut into large chunks
1 x 140-g/5-oz. can pineapple pieces in juice (reserve the juice for the sauce)

FOR THE SAUCE
2 tablespoons tomato ketchup
3 tablespoons rice vinegar
1 teaspoon tomato purée/paste
1 tablespoon Hendersons relish or vegan Worcestershire sauce
3 teaspoons potato starch, or cornflour/cornstarch
3 tablespoons agave syrup
80 ml/⅓ cup pineapple juice (leftover from the can, see left)

SERVES 4

Put all the ingredients for the sauce in a small pan and whisk well. Place on a medium heat and bring to a simmer, whisking regularly to ensure a smooth sauce. Once the sauce is simmering, remove from the heat and set aside.

Heat the oil for frying in a small wok over a medium-high heat to approximately 180°C/350°F (to test the temperature, drop a small crumb of bread into the oil; if it sizzles and floats without burning, the oil is ready to use). Pat the mock pork dry and chop into bite-sized pieces. Put the pieces in a small bowl and add the potato starch or cornflour/cornstarch, white pepper and 1 teaspoon of the salt and mix well. Put the vegan 'egg' substitute in another small bowl. Lift the pieces from the flour and dip in the 'egg' substitute. Dip into the flour again. Repeat the process to get a nice chewy coating on the 'pork' pieces. Place on some greaseproof paper. Fry the pieces in batches, for about 5–6 minutes, until the pieces float and the batter is crispy. Drain on paper towels and set aside.

In a large wok or frying pan/skillet, add the tablespoon of vegetable or sesame oil and put over a high heat. When the pan is hot, add the onion and (bell) peppers and stir-fry for several minutes. Add the pineapple and the sauce. Bring to a simmer, then add the fried mock pork and season with the remaining salt, to taste. Mix well to ensure everything is well coated and then simmer for a few minutes until the fried pieces start to soften and become chewier. Serve with steamed rice.

PHAD SEE EEW JAY
THAI FRIED WIDE NOODLES WITH GREENS & CASHEWS

Any kind of Thai noodles are always a family crowd-pleaser in our house. This dish makes a nice change from Phad Thai Jay and is super easy to make. The traditional choice of noodle is the very wide, flat rice noodles, but you can also use small noodle sheets or indeed any noodles you like. Leafy greens are an essential ingredient, but you can substitute the Chinese broccoli for big leafy spinach, chard or pak choi/bok choy. Mangetout/snow peas and broccoli also make great additional vegetables. You can buy ready-made tofu puffs from the Chinese supermarket to save time, instead of making your own. I make them in batches and then freeze ready to use later.

300 g/10½ oz. flat, wide rice noodles (sen yai or chow fun in Chinese)

2 tablespoons vegetable oil, plus extra for frying

1 x 396-g/14-oz. packet firm tofu, excess water drained

4 tablespoons plain/all-purpose flour

1 x 280-g/10-oz. can fried gluten mock chicken, drained and rinsed

6 garlic cloves, crushed

2 large handfuls of leafy greens, such as Chinese broccoli or pak choi/bok choy, choi sum, etc., roughly chopped

FOR THE SAUCE

6 tablespoons soy sauce

3 tablespoons kecap manis (dark sweet soy sauce)

½–1 teaspoon unrefined sugar or agave syrup, to taste

1½ tablespoons rice vinegar

1 teaspoon sea salt

1 teaspoon ground white pepper

TO SERVE

1 teaspoon dried chilli/hot red pepper flakes

handful of toasted cashews

SERVES 4

Soak the noodles in almost-boiling water for 15–20 minutes until completely softened. Drain and set aside.

Mix together all the sauce ingredients in a jug/pitcher, stirring well until all the salt and sugar have dissolved. Taste and adjust the seasoning as needed.

In a small pan, add about 4–5 cm/1½–2 inches of oil and place on a medium-high heat. Halve the tofu block and cut one half into cubes. Toss the cubes in the flour, then place gently in the hot oil. Fry until just crisp, then put onto paper towels to drain. Cut the mock chicken into large bite-sized pieces.

Put the crushed garlic into a large wok or frying pan/skillet, with the 2 tablespoons of oil. Crumble the remaining tofu into the pan, mix well and stir-fry for a few minutes over a medium-high heat. Add the mock chicken pieces, the greens and half of the sauce. Stir-fry for about 3–4 minutes, then add the noodles, fried tofu cubes and remaining sauce. Toss well so all the noodles are well coated. Serve immediately, with a sprinkle of dried chilli/hot red pepper flakes and cashews.

SESAME RICE BALLS
STUFFED WITH OYSTER MUSHROOM 'BULGOGI' & KIMCHI

This is a great recipe for using up leftover rice, especially sticky rice. Deep-fried rice balls are a staple in South East Asian food halls for this very reason. This recipe is inspired by the confident American fusion cooking I came to love on my travels there.

FOR THE RICE
150 g/5½ oz. glutinous rice
1 tablespoon Thai rice, Berry rice or substitute black or wild rice
1 teaspoon sea salt

FOR THE FILLING
60 g/2¼ oz. fresh oyster mushrooms, cleaned and roughly chopped
1 tablespoon toasted sesame oil
1 tablespoon vegetable oil
1 small banana shallot, finely diced
¼ small carrot, peeled and finely diced
1 spring onion/scallion, thinly sliced

FOR THE MARINADE
4 tablespoons soy sauce
3 tablespoons brown sugar
2 tablespoons rice wine
1 small onion, grated
2 garlic cloves, finely chopped
1 teaspoon ginger paste
¼ Granny Smith apple, cored and grated
½ teaspoon salt
½ teaspoon freshly ground black pepper

TO ASSEMBLE
200 g/1½ cups white sesame seeds
2 teaspoons black sesame seeds (optional)
6–8 tablespoons aquafaba 'egg' (see page 12), or substitute other vegan 'egg', such as flax egg or Orgran
2 tablespoons vegan kimchi, chopped
salt and white pepper
oil for deep frying, such as sunflower or rapeseed

MAKES 4–5 LARGE BALLS

Soak all the rice in warm water for at least 3 hours. Rinse and drain. Put the rice in a rice steamer or pan with the salt and 500 ml/2 cups plus 2 tablespoons water. If cooking in a pan, bring to the boil without the lid and simmer until almost all the water is absorbed. Remove from the heat and cover with a clean kitchen towel and lid. Set aside to steam for a further 10–15 minutes. Once the rice is cooked, set aside to cool or refrigerate overnight.

Mix all the marinade ingredients together in a small bowl. Add the oyster mushrooms and combine well. Cover and refrigerate for 1 hour or so.

In a deep frying pan/skillet, add the toasted sesame oil, vegetable oil, shallot, carrot and spring onion/scallion and put over a medium-high heat. Cook for a few minutes, then add the oyster mushrooms, leaving any excess marinade in the bowl. Cook over a high heat for 8–10 minutes. Set aside.

Put all the sesame seeds and some salt and pepper on a large plate and put the aquafaba or vegan 'egg' substitute in a small bowl.

Wet your hands and take a handful of sticky rice. Shape into a deep saucer in one hand. Put a small spoonful of the mushroom mixture into the hollow centre. Top with a pinch of kimchi and fold over the sides of the rice to make a large ball. Roll the ball in your hands to ensure the edges are well sealed. Roll the rice ball in the aquafaba or vegan 'egg' substitute, then in the sesame seeds. Repeat to ensure a thick crust of sesame seeds. Put on a sheet of greaseproof paper and repeat with the remaining rice.

Heat the oil in a deep pan to 175°C/325°F. Fry the balls in small batches for 3–4 minutes on each side, until crispy all over. Drain on paper towels. Serve warm with any leftover marinade, extra kimchi and hoisin.

CHOW ROLL
GIANT SPRING ROLL STUFFED
WITH MOCK CHICKEN CHOW MEIN

In between writing cookery books and teaching, I also work as a development chef. My work with Tampopo, Manchester's iconic Pan-Asian restaurant group, began with a joint pop-up dining event for the local Food & Drink Festival in 2011. This is one of the recipes that didn't quite make it to the service frontline. It's an easy dish to make, but just not in excessively large quantities. The chow mein itself has become one of their best-selling dishes. The street food chef in me can never resist a dish that can be eaten single-handed!

1 tablespoon vegetable oil

3 garlic cloves, crushed

handful of shredded white cabbage

handful of chopped pak choi/bok choy or other greens

handful of beansprouts

2 spring onions/scallions, trimmed and thinly sliced

1 carrot, peeled and grated

60 g/¼ cup bamboo shoot matchsticks, drained and rinsed

1 x 280-g/10-oz. can fried gluten/mock chicken, drained and rinsed, or 240 g/8¾ oz. fragrant satay 'chicken' (see page 41), chopped into small pieces

approx. 200 g/7 oz. dried yellow egg-free noodles, soaked in hot water for 20–30 minutes and drained

12 sheets of 30-cm/ 12-inch spring roll wrappers

vegetable oil, for brushing

soy sauce or kecap manis, to serve

FOR THE SAUCE

1 tablespoon soy sauce

3 tablespoons vegetarian oyster/stir-fry sauce

2 tablespoons Shaoxing rice wine

2 teaspoons sugar

½–1 teaspoon salt

1 teaspoon toasted sesame oil

½ teaspoon ground white pepper

MAKES 4 LARGE ROLLS

Preheat the oven to 180°C (350°F) Gas 4. To make the sauce, whisk all the ingredients together, stirring well until the sugar and salt have fully dissolved.

Put the vegetable oil into a large wok over a medium-high heat. Add the garlic and fry until crispy. Next, add the vegetables and stir-fry for 1–2 minutes. Add half the sauce and all the mock chicken pieces and mix well. Add the noodles and, using large chopsticks or paddles, toss and mix the noodles well with all the vegetables and the remaining sauce. Once everything is well coated, remove from the heat and add 1–2 tablespoons of cold water if needed to ensure the noodles are nice and slippery. Set aside.

Take a spring roll wrapper and brush well with oil. Fill the lower centre half with the chow mein noodle mixture. Start by rolling the wrapper away from you, halfway folding in the ends to make a snug parcel, and roll the last part to the end and then brush the ends with oil to seal. Lay the roll across another wrapper diagonally and roll halfway, fold in the sides and roll to the end. Try to roll firmly but not too tightly or they will burst when cooking. You may need to wrap a third wrapper around the noodle roll to ensure they are snugly wrapped. Repeat to make a further three rolls. Brush generously with oil and lay on a baking sheet. Bake in the preheated oven for 20–25 minutes, turning several times to ensure even baking, until crispy and golden brown.

Serve immediately with soy sauce or kecap manis for dipping.

SIZZLING DRUMSTICKS

Mimicking a meat-based dish to this extent, as with the vegan belly bits recipe (see page 38), may not be to everyone's taste. However, I stand by this dish knowing that committed meat-eaters have thoroughly enjoyed this, and thus going some way to help in moving their choices to plant-based dishes that have real bite, instead of eating meat. You could certainly serve these drumsticks with alternative sauces, such as sweet and sour (see page 22) or peanut sauce (see page 43). This recipe uses my favourite Thai-inspired sticky sauce with crunchy cashews.

¼ packet fresh or dried bean curd sheets/skins (approx. 75 g/2½ oz.), cut into 6 oblong sheets (approx. 12.5 x 7.5 cm/5 x 3 inches)
1 litre/1 quart boiling vegetable stock
2 x 280-g/10-oz. cans gluten/seitan mock chicken, drained and rinsed, or use Vietnamese 'chicken ham' (see page 14)
1 tablespoon vegetable oil
4 tablespoons soy sauce

FOR THE SAUCE
6 large red chillies/chiles, finely chopped
6 garlic cloves, finely chopped
½ teaspoon ground white pepper
2 tablespoons Shaoxing rice wine or cooking sherry
2 tablespoons dark soy sauce
4 tablespoons agave syrup
½–1 tablespoon brown sugar, to taste
1 tablespoon freshly squeezed lime juice
½ teaspoon sea salt
large handful of fresh coriander/cilantro, finely chopped

TO SERVE
handful of toasted cashews, roughly chopped
handful of spring onions/scallions, thinly sliced at an angle
freshly chopped coriander/cilantro and sliced red chilli/chile, to garnish (optional)

6 x 8-cm/3-inch lolly/popsicle sticks
cast-iron skillet or sizzling platter

MAKES 6 DRUMSTICKS

Lay the bean curd sheets in a large, wide dish, cover with the hot stock and soak for a few minutes.

Mix all the ingredients for the sauce together in a large bowl and set aside for 10 minutes.

Preheat the oven to 185°C (350°F) Gas 4.

Slice the mock chicken into large oblong pieces, 5 x 2.5 x 1 cm/2 x 1 x ½ inch (make them slightly wider at one end for a better drumstick shape). Gently slide a lolly/popsicle stick into the narrower end of each piece, so 2.5 cm/1 inch of the stick is inside the piece.

Take a softened bean curd sheet/skin and place on a flat surface. Lay the mock chicken piece with an inserted stick at one corner of the sheet. Roll the piece in the bean curd sheet, folding in the top at the widest end, to make a broadly triangular shape. Roll firmly but not too tightly or the curd will split. Brush with oil to seal and place on a lightly oiled baking sheet to set slightly. Brush with soy sauce. Repeat with all the pieces to make approximately 6 drumsticks.

Bake in the preheated oven for 15–20 minutes until the outsides are crispy and browning. Remove from the oven and set aside.

Heat the skillet or sizzling platter over a high heat, either in the oven or on the hob/stovetop, for about 10 minutes. Carefully remove and place on a heatproof board or block. Lay the drumsticks onto the platter and pour over the sauce, taking care not to get splashed by the sizzling platter. Serve immediately, scattering the top with cashews, spring onions/scallions, coriander/cilantro and extra chilli/chile if you like.

BAO ZI
STEAMED BUNS WITH BARBECUED JACKFRUIT & PICKLED CUCUMBER

I love a good steamed bun (or bao) and I've eaten my fair share of vegan beauties over the years. They seem to appear quite often in the food halls of Asian malls, but the filling has never really wowed me. Especially not in the way that my omni friends are wowed by British Street Food Award winners Yum Bun or SoHo's Bao. The vegan filling can sometimes be too carby or simply not salty or sharp enough to compliment the fluffy but plain bun. Green jackfruit makes an excellent base to build on with some sweet, salty and tangy flavours. And the quick pickled cucumber adds the perfect little crunch.

FOR THE QUICK PICKLED CUCUMBER
- ½ cucumber, washed and thinly sliced
- 3 tablespoons rice vinegar
- 2 tablespoons caster/granulated sugar
- 1 star anise, bruised

FOR THE STEAMED BUNS
- 500 g/3⅔ cups strong white bread flour
- 2 tablespoons caster/superfine sugar
- 7 g sachet/2 teaspoons fast-acting dried yeast
- ½ teaspoon baking powder
- ½ teaspoon sea salt
- 145 ml/scant ⅔ cup lukewarm water
- 145 ml/scant ⅔ cup soy milk
- 1 tablespoon coconut oil, melted
- vegetable oil, for greasing and brushing

FOR THE FILLING
- 1 x 565-g/20-oz. can green jackfruit, drained and rinsed
- 4–5 garlic cloves, finely chopped
- 1 x 60-g/2-oz. piece of fresh ginger, peeled and finely chopped
- 2 tablespoons vegetable oil
- 2 tablespoons tomato ketchup
- 5 tablespoons hoisin sauce
- 2–3 tablespoons caster/granulated sugar
- 2 tablespoons dark soy sauce
- 2 tablespoons rice vinegar

TO SERVE
- 1 spring onion/scallion, trimmed and thinly sliced at an angle
- handful of fresh coriander/cilantro
- 1 tablespoon crushed toasted peanuts (optional)

MAKES APPROX. 12–14

To make the quick pickled cucumber, add all the ingredients to a small bowl and mix well. Set aside.

Mix together all the ingredients for the steamed buns, except the vegetable oil. Knead well using a machine fitted with a dough hook or by hand until it all comes together to make a smooth dough. Place the dough in a well-oiled bowl and cover with clingfilm/plastic wrap. Leave to rest for about 1 hour in a warm place, until doubled in size.

Remove the dough and roll into a giant sausage shape. Divide into approximately 12–14 portions and roll into balls. Using a rolling pin, flatten each ball into an oval. Brush with oil, fold the oval gently in half and place on a well-oiled baking sheet. Rest the buns in a warm place for 30 minutes until risen again.

Prepare the steamer by placing greaseproof paper on the layers and lightly oiling. Put the steamer over a pan of water and bring to the boil. Gently place the buns into the steamer, evenly spaced, and steam for 15–20 minutes. The buns will rise and have a slight bounce when prodded. Set aside.

To make the filling, place all the ingredients in a small pan and bring to a simmer. Cook gently on a low heat for 20–25 minutes until the jackfruit is completely softened. Add a splash of water if the mixture is too dry – it should be soft and sticky-looking. Use a wooden spoon to break up the jackfruit. Fill the buns with a layer of pickled cucumber, a spoonful of jackfruit mixture, spring onion/scallion, coriander/cilantro and a sprinkle of peanuts, if using.

BACON-WRAPPED MUSHROOM SKEWERS

Wrapping bacon around mushrooms should be exactly as easy as it sounds. With most vegan options it's rarely so simple, but using a ready-made vegan rasher alternative means it can be. If I'm using ready-made, I use Sgaia Mheats streaky rashers or I pick up one from the Chinese supermarket that looks like a block of pork belly (kind of), and slice it with a very sharp knife. Alternatively, make your own batch of mock smoky 'bacon' (page 12) and freeze what you don't use.

1 bunch enoki
    mushrooms, approx.
    250 g/9 oz.
12 rashers/slices mock
    smoky bacon (see
    page 12) or 12 rashers/
    slices ready-made
    vegan bacon

FOR THE MARINADE
2 tablespoons tomato
    ketchup
2 tablespoons brown
    sauce

4 small bamboo skewers,
    soaked in water
lightly oiled baking sheet

MAKES 4 APPETIZER-SIZE
SKEWERS

First make the marinade. Mix together the tomato ketchup and brown sauce in a small bowl.

Clean and trim the enoki mushrooms. Lay on a chopping board and slice the enoki into small 2-cm/¾-inch clumps (preferably still held together at the bottom).

Unwrap the mock smoky bacon dough and using a very sharp large knife, slice the dough to make long, thin rasher-like strips. You can freeze the sliced pieces, and use as needed for other bacon dishes.

Lay a slice on the chopping board, then place a small clump of enoki at one end and roll the slice up to enclose the enoki. Slide onto a skewer to fix in place. Repeat so there are three or four rolls on each skewer.

Lightly brush the skewers with the marinade and lay on a lightly oiled baking sheet. Place under a preheated hot grill/broiler and cook for a few minutes on each side, until they are starting to crisp and brown. Serve immediately.

PANANG CURRY
WITH FRAGRANT 'CHICKEN' & PEA AUBERGINES

This dish might be in the running, along with Rendang and Khao Soi Curry Noodles (both in my book *Vegan Street Food*), for South East Asia's biggest crowd-pleasing curry. This thick, salty and sweet Thai curry is rarely made with vegetables, and usually with beef, pork or chicken. Sometimes the small Thai pea aubergines/eggplants are added, but you could substitute with green peas if you like.

This recipe uses the fragrant chicken-like seitan recipe but you could use any ready-made vegan chicken pieces. Simply add the bite-sized pieces into the rich curry sauce. You could also use ready-made canned seitan from a Chinese supermarket. Ensure the pieces are well rinsed in warm water and dried before using, or the flavour of the brine will dominate the sauce. Simply use your hands to tear the pieces into the curry during the last few minutes of simmering.

FOR THE PANANG PASTE
1 teaspoon ground cumin
1 teaspoon freshly ground black pepper
1 teaspoon ground coriander
3 lemongrass stalks, trimmed
5 kaffir lime leaves
4 garlic cloves, peeled
4–5-cm/1½–2-inch piece of fresh galangal (or use fresh ginger), peeled
4 banana shallots, peeled
10 small red bird's eye chillies/chiles
3 large red chillies/chiles
2 tablespoons soy sauce
½–1 teaspoon sea salt, to taste
3 tablespoons red-skinned peanuts, lightly toasted, plus extra to garnish
1–2 tablespoons vegetable oil

FOR THE CURRY
1 x 400-ml/14-oz. can coconut milk
1½ tablespoons soft dark brown sugar
1 teaspoon ground white pepper
large handful of fresh Thai pea aubergines/eggplants (or use frozen peas)
320 g/11½ oz. fragrant satay 'chicken' pieces (see page 41)
½–1 teaspoon sea salt, to taste
2 limes, 1 cut into wedges

SERVES 4–6

For the paste, gently toast the cumin, black pepper and coriander in a small frying pan/skillet until they start to smell fragrant. Take care not to burn them or they will taste bitter. Add all the Panang paste ingredients into a blender, including the toasted spices, and blitz to make a smooth paste. Add a little of the vegetable oil if needed to loosen the mixture and ensure everything blends evenly.

Place a heavy-based pan over a medium heat and then add 4 tablespoons of the paste to the pan along with a tablespoon of the oil. Cook the paste gently for 8–9 minutes. (Any unused paste will keep in an airtight container in the fridge for a week, or can be frozen.)

Add the coconut milk, sugar and white pepper to the pan, then bring to a simmer and cook on a low heat for approximately 10 minutes, then add the pea aubergines/eggplants and cook for further 20–30 minutes until well thickened. Next, add the 'chicken' pieces (and frozen peas if using instead of pea aubergines/eggplants) and bring to a simmer again. Check the seasoning, and add more salt and sugar to taste. Finish with the juice of one lime.

Serve with steamed jasmine rice, a wedge of lime and a sprinkle of toasted nuts, if you like.

VEGAN BELLY BITS

Spare ribs and pork belly are dishes I know some of my vegetarian friends miss, because we've gone in search of mock versions ever since we ate our first mock ribs at a Chinese restaurant on Manchester's Portland St. The Hong Pat was a standard yet unique Chinese restaurant, that sadly closed its doors in the late 90s and got replaced by an off-licence. Our little gang of vegetarians used to love that place with a passion. Not least for the mock spare ribs, sweet and sour mock pork and nutty lettuce wraps they served alongside their standard UK-Cantonese fayre.

Over a decade later, I found myself searching for a Buddhist Chinese restaurant around the back streets of Kuala Lumpur, because I had heard from a vegetarian friend who had moved to KL that there was some truly great mock meat to be had. My children were only seven years old and I insisted on walking, since I only had a vague idea of where it might be, and worried we would miss it from the back of a taxi. So we walked and walked in the late afternoon heat, and everyone got a bit cross with me. But we eventually found Fat Yan's – and it was worth all the smoggy traffic dodging because we found an absolute gem. To the children's insistence, we ate there several times every time we came through KL and the restaurant staff even remembered us when we returned after several years, giving the children bracelets to protect them on their journeys. Unfortunately time catches up with all of these places, and this too has since been replaced with a standard non-vegetarian Chinese restaurant.

Skip forward another 10 years and I'm in Portland, Oregon. And thanks to the wonder that is online restaurant research, I found a vegan Vietnamese café run by Buddhist nuns, somewhere on the outskirts of the city. I could see my omni-travel buddy Maya was about as excited about this prospect as my children were when I made them walk across KL in the afternoon heat. I pleaded with her to come, promising that the joys of mock meat would be revealed in all their glory. Suffice to say she was not disappointed.

75 ml/⅓ cup coconut cream
1½ tablespoons tapioca starch
5–6 large pieces of Vietnamese vegan 'chicken ham', approx. 5–7.5 cm/2–3 inches wide and 2.5–5 cm/1–2 inches thick (see page 14) (approx. ½ ready-made roll)
¼ baguette
2 tablespoons coconut oil

FOR THE SAUCE
1 teaspoon five spice powder
2 tablespoons soy sauce
½ teaspoon sesame oil
3 tablespoons soft dark brown sugar or agave syrup

12 pieces of greaseproof paper cut into large rectangles, or banana leaves soaked in hot water
twine

SERVES 2–4

In a small pan, add all the ingredients for the sauce plus 1 tablespoon water and whisk well. Place on a medium heat and bring to a simmer, with regular whisking to ensure a smooth sauce. Once the sauce is simmering for a few minutes and nicely thickened, remove from the heat and set aside.

In another small pan, add the coconut cream and whisk in the tapioca starch. Place on a low heat and bring to a gentle simmer, stirring, until the mixture thickens. Remove from the heat and set aside.

Place the 'chicken ham' pieces into a bowl and pour over three-quarters of the sticky barbecue sauce from the pan. Mix well, taking care not to break the pieces. Leave to marinate for 10 minutes.

Slice the baguette in half lengthways. Using a spoon or your hands, scrape out and discard the excess bread inside leaving only the crust. Slice the baguette crust into large oblongs (you need 5 or 6 in total), to fit the wide top of the marinated pieces. Spread the inside of the crust pieces with a teaspoon of the coconut cream mixture on each.

Lay two rectangles of greaseproof paper on a board (you can also use banana leaves, if you prefer), then place a crust in the centre, coconut cream facing upwards. Next, put a piece of the marinated 'chicken ham' into the centre. Fold and wrap over the sides of the greaseproof paper to make a small, tight parcel. Tie with twine to secure. Repeat the process with all the pieces of 'chicken ham'.

Place the parcels into a steamer, and cook for 20–30 minutes. Remove from the steamer and remove the paper carefully. Leave to cool and dry slightly, for approximately 20–30 minutes. Brush with a little more sauce on top.

In a large frying pan/skillet, add 2 tablespoons coconut oil and place over a medium-high heat. Add the unwrapped parcels and sear on all sides to caramelize well, frying in batches of 4 or 5. Lay on a baking sheet and keep warm in a low oven until all the pieces are cooked. Drizzle the cooked pieces with any leftover sauce before serving.

GILI GADO NOODLE SOUP
WITH FRAGRANT SATAY 'CHICKEN' SKEWERS

The trio of Gili Islands sits off the north-west corner of Lombok, an Indonesian island near Bali. These fantasy islands were once a sleepy idyll of pony carts (no motorized vehicles allowed) and world-class snorkelling, and I'm thankful for all the time we spent there as a family and learning to free-dive like a local. The area became more famous following the novel *Eat, Pray, Love* and is now firmly on every backpacker's hit list. And for good reason. The Gili Islands are Indonesia's answer to what paradise might look like, and are a haven for turtles and now tourists alike.

I doubt any tourists leave the Gili Islands without eating Gado-Gado at least once, with its famous spicy peanut sauce (drizzled over cooked and raw vegetables). This recipe brings together some of my favourite Indonesian flavours. You can also save lots of time and use pieces of tempeh or tofu instead of these fragrant little bites, but there are lots of other ways to use this fragrantly-spiced mock chicken, such as Panang Curry (see page 37), Chow Roll (see page 29) or even sliced into a sandwich. The skewers can be served as an appetizer with the peanut dip, and make a great party food too.

FOR THE BRAISING STOCK
1 sheet of kombu seaweed, broken into pieces and soaked in cold water for 20 minutes
2 litres/8½ cups good-quality vegetable stock
2 lemongrass stalks, ends well crushed
1 x 6–7-cm/2½–2¾ inch thumb of fresh ginger, peeled and thinly sliced
4 dried mushrooms, such as porcini or shiitake
120 ml/½ cup soy sauce

FOR THE FRAGRANT SATAY 'CHICKEN'
2 tablespoons sesame oil
1 small leek, finely chopped
6 spring onions/scallions, trimmed and thinly sliced
4 garlic cloves, finely chopped
2 lemongrass stalks, fat half only, smashed and then finely chopped (add the rest to the broth)
3 teaspoons ground coriander
½–1 teaspoon sea salt, to taste
200 g/7 oz. vital wheat gluten flour
1½ tablespoons chickpea/gram flour
2 tablespoons soy sauce
4–5 tablespoons vegetable oil

First, rinse the kombu and add to a large pan along with all the other braising stock ingredients. Bring to the boil and then simmer on a low heat, covered, for 1 hour. Remove the lid and leave to cool. Strain the broth through a fine sieve/strainer. This stock can be frozen in portions for later use.

To make the fragrant satay 'chicken', add the sesame oil to a small frying pan/skillet and place on a medium heat. Add the leek and spring onions/scallions. Sauté for 5–6 minutes until softened. Add the garlic, lemongrass, ground coriander and salt. Stir well and sauté for another 5–6 minutes. Set aside.

Place the wheat gluten and chickpea/gram flours in a large bowl, then add the leek mixture from the pan along with 235 ml/1 cup of the stock and the soy sauce. Using gloved hands, mix well and add more stock as needed to make a firm dough. Roll out the dough into two long, thick sausage shapes.

Lay out a large piece of muslin/cheesecloth on the work surface. Generously oil the cloth. Place one of the sausage shapes onto the cloth, then roll up tightly and tie at each end like a giant Christmas cracker. Wrap some extra twine around the middle to ensure the dough is snugly wrapped in the cloth.

FOR THE PEANUT SAUCE

2 tablespoons coconut oil
4 garlic cloves, finely
  chopped
1 tablespoon finely
  chopped fresh ginger
  or 2 teaspoons ground
  ginger
2–3 teaspoons dried chilli
  flakes/hot red pepper
  flakes
3 heaped teaspoons
  garam masala
8 generous tablespoons
  crunchy peanut butter
  (if sugar-free, add
  1 tablespoon unrefined
  sugar or agave syrup)
200 ml/generous ¾ cup
  coconut milk
1–2 teaspoons sea salt,
  to taste

TO SERVE

2 large handfuls of
  beansprouts
1 large handful of fresh
  greens, such as kale,
  roughly chopped
200 g/7 oz. dried yellow
  egg-free noodles,
  soaked in hot water
  for 15–20 minutes,
  then drained
½ cucumber, deseeded
  and cut into 5-cm/
  2-inch batons
red chillies/chiles,
  roughly chopped
fresh coriander/cilantro,
  roughly torn
lime wedges
2 tablespoons chilli/
  chile sambal, to serve
  (optional)

muslin/cheesecloth
twine
8 bamboo skewers,
  soaked in cold water

SERVES 4

Repeat with the second piece of dough. Now add 1 litre/1 quart of the stock to a large pan and bring to a simmer. Add the wrapped seitan doughs and bring to boil again. Simmer for about 1 hour, then remove from the pan and set aside to cool.

Once these are cooled, unwrap and, using a sharp knife, cut a thick slice, then halve this piece to form large bite-sized chunks to fit on the skewer. Thread 3–4 pieces onto each skewer and set aside.

For the peanut sauce, in a medium pan, add the coconut oil and place on a medium–high heat. Add the garlic and ginger and fry until starting to soften, then add the dried chilli/hot red pepper flakes and garam masala. Add a tablespoon of water and the peanut butter, then stir well until the mixture starts to simmer. Cook on a low heat for a few minutes. The sauce should be sticky and thick. Set aside.

Generously coat the skewers with some of the peanut sauce and lay on a lightly oiled baking sheet. Place under a preheated hot grill/broiler and cook for a few minutes on each side until nicely browned.

In a medium pan, add 400 ml/1¾ cups of the remaining stock plus the remaining peanut sauce and coconut milk. Bring to a simmer, then season to taste with salt. The broth should be fairly soupy, but not too thin. Add a little more water or reduce if needed. Add the beansprouts and greens, and bring back to a simmer. Then add the softened noodles just for a moment to reheat them, and ladle the soupy noodles into big bowls. Serve each bowl of soup with one or two skewers, along with a handful of cucumber batons, a squeeze of lime and scatter on fresh chillies/chiles and coriander/cilantro leaves if you like. Serve some hot sambal on the side for an extra kick if you wish.

BUN BO HUE CHAY
VIETNAMESE SPICY NOODLE SOUP WITH 'CHICKEN HAM'

This is an 'involved recipe', but well worth the effort for this big bowl of spicy comforting noodles. Vietnamese soup noodles are often made with bone-based broths, but this vegan version is equally fierce and deep in umami.

FOR THE BROTH
3 lemongrass stalks
1 leek
10-cm/4-inch piece of fresh ginger, peeled and thinly sliced
1 large onion, quartered
½ fresh pineapple, peeled, cored and cut into chunks (or use 1 x 227-g/8-oz. can pineapple in juice, not syrup, drained)
2 Granny Smith apples, cored, peeled and roughly cut into chunks
5 dried shiitake mushrooms (preferably good-quality Japanese ones) or use 20 g/¾ oz. dried wild mushrooms
350 g/12 oz. mooli/daikon radishes, peeled and roughly sliced
½ Chinese leaf/napa cabbage, thinly sliced (or use white cabbage)
1 litre/1 quart good-quality vegetable stock or use 1 tablespoon good-quality bouillon and water

FOR THE SAUCE
2 tablespoons coconut or vegetable oil
1 large bulb of garlic, roasted whole until soft, then peeled and crushed

3 tablespoons fermented bean curd pieces and 1 tablespoon sauce from jar (chao)
3 tablespoons fermented soy bean paste (mam ruoc chay), to taste
1 tablespoon Korean red chilli/hot pepper flakes
1 tablespoon smoked paprika

TO SERVE
8 fried tofu puffs, halved
250 g/9 oz. rice vermicelli noodles, soaked in boiling water for 10–15 minutes, then drained
¼ white cabbage, thinly sliced
¼ red cabbage, thinly sliced
6 spring onions/scallions, thinly sliced at an angle
large handful of beansprouts
6 x 5-mm/¼-inch slices of Vietnamese vegan 'chicken ham' roll (see page 14), halved again into half-moon shapes
2–3 sprigs of fresh lemon thyme, finely chopped
handful of freshly chopped mint
handful of freshly chopped coriander/cilantro

SERVES 4–6

Remove the ends of the lemongrass stalks and discard the outer layers. Cut the lemongrass stalks in half and separate the white thick stalks from the greener ends. Bruise, crush and finely chop the white parts and set aside. Bruise the green ends and put in a large stock pan. Cut the leek in half, roughly chop the dark green part and add to the pan. Finely chop the white part and set aside. Add the ginger, onion, fruit, mushrooms, mooli/daikon, cabbage and stock to the large stock pan, plus 2.5 litres/11 cups of water. Bring to the boil over a high heat and then reduce to a simmer. Skim off any foamy scum and simmer for about 1½ hours. Remove from the heat and leave to cool for about 10–20 minutes, then strain the broth. Keep the mushrooms and discard the other vegetables. Chop the mushrooms and set aside.

For the sauce, place a frying pan/skillet over a medium heat, add the white parts of the lemongrass and oil and fry gently for 2 minutes. Add the remaining ingredients. Stir well, cooking gently for a couple of minutes, then remove from the heat and set aside.

Return the broth to a large deep pan (using as much as you need to fill 4–6 big bowls – any leftovers can be chilled for up to a week or frozen). Place the pan over a high heat and bring to a simmer, adding the tofu puffs, reserved mushrooms and two-thirds of the sauce. Stir well and remove from the heat. Adjust the seasoning and add more paste if desired. To serve, place a handful of noodles into each bowl and top with small handfuls of the cabbage, spring onions/scallions, beansprouts, ham roll slices and herbs. Ladle over the broth, distributing the tofu and mushrooms between the bowls. Scatter the remaining herbs and shredded white leek on top. Serve with more cabbage, beansprouts and sauce.

MA PO TOFU
WITH WILD MUSHROOMS

Ma-Po was the wife of a Sichuan chef who created this dish over 150 years ago, and it's widely written that the popularity of the dish is not least due to the affordability of tofu over meat. It was not uncommon for meat to be omitted or replaced with mushrooms and other fungi. Being a relatively simple dish of meaty substance, vegetarian versions have also been long favoured during the observance of zhai jie, the Buddhist practice of a vegan diet – which many meat eaters practise during Uposatha – a bit like Sabbath days in Christianity and Judaism or Ramadan in Islam, where people may choose to intensify their practices and ethics.

3 tablespoons Sichuan peppercorns

3 tablespoons vegetable oil

400-g/14-oz. block of medium-firm or silken tofu, cut into bite-sized cubes

2 level teaspoons cornflour/cornstarch or potato starch

35 g/1¼ oz. assorted dried wild mushrooms, soaked in boiling water for 10 minutes, then drained and chopped

125 g/4½ oz. fresh oyster mushrooms, roughly chopped

¼ teaspoon sesame oil

4 garlic cloves, thinly sliced

5-cm/2-inch piece of fresh ginger, finely chopped

1 tablespoon fermented black beans (or use 2 tablespoons black bean sauce)

1 tablespoon dark soy sauce

2 tablespoons fermented chilli bean paste (or use fermented broad bean paste, slightly less spicy but easier to find)

2 tablespoons Shaoxing wine or dry sherry

4 tablespoons roasted chilli/chili oil (type with a dark red colour)

6 tablespoons vegetable stock

½ teaspoon coarsely ground black pepper

½–1 teaspoon sea salt, to taste

3 spring onions/scallions, thinly sliced at an angle

SERVES 3–4

Place a large dry wok on a high heat and heat until smoking. Add half the peppercorns and dry-toast for a few moments until lightly roasted, then transfer to a mortar and grind well. Set aside to use before serving.

Add the remaining peppercorns to the pan along with the vegetable oil and sizzle on high for 1–2 minutes. Remove the peppercorns from the oil and discard. Add the tofu pieces into the spiced oil, and fry until crisped slightly, but take care not to break up the pieces. Better to toss the wok here rather than using tongs. Remove the tofu and set aside on a plate.

Combine the cornflour/cornstarch with a little splash of water and mix to make a paste. Set aside.

Add all the mushrooms and the sesame oil to the remaining oil in the wok, return to a high heat and cook for a minute. Once it starts smoking, add the garlic and ginger, and keep tossing on a high heat for another 30 seconds. Add the remaining ingredients, except the tofu and spring onions/scallions. Mix well and then add the cornflour/cornstarch paste, and cook for another minute until slightly thickened. The sauce should be a velvety pouring consistency. Add a little more water if the sauce is too thick. Taste and season with more salt according to taste. Gently fold in the tofu, half of the Sichuan pepper powder and half of the spring onions/scallions.

To serve, scatter with the remaining spring onions/scallions and a few pinches of the remaining toasted Sichuan pepper and serve with steamed rice.

CHKN KATSU CURRY

In language terms, katsu refers to a flattened escalope, which is breaded with panko and fried; it's most often served with a tangy and sweet Japanese curry sauce. I make larger quantities of this spice mix and keep it in the cupboard labelled as 'Japanese masala'.

FOR THE 'JAPANESE MASALA' SPICE MIX
3 teaspoons ground turmeric
3 teaspoons ground coriander
1½ teaspoons ground cumin
1 scant teaspoon green cardamom seeds, ground to a powder
½ teaspoon freshly ground black pepper
¼ teaspoon ground white pepper
1 clove, ground to a powder
¼ teaspoon fennel powder
tiny pinch of ground cinnamon (optional)
¼ teaspoon hot chilli/chili powder

FOR THE CURRY ROUX
4 tablespoons olive oil
30 g/3⅔ tablespoons plain/all-purpose flour
2 generous tablespoons Japanese Masala spice mix (see above)
½ teaspoon mild chilli/chili powder
1 tablespoon tomato ketchup
1 tablespoon brown sauce

FOR THE ONION STOCK
1–2 tablespoons vegetable oil
2 large onions, thinly sliced
1 small carrot, peeled and roughly chopped
800 ml/3⅓ cups light vegetable stock
1 small banana, roughly chopped
2 teaspoons sea salt
1 teaspoon Japanese Masala spice mix (see left)

FOR THE BREADED 'KATSU'
100 g/¾ cup plain/all-purpose flour
1 teaspoon sea salt
1 teaspoon ground white pepper
8 tablespoons aquafaba (see page 12) or other vegan 'egg' substitute, such as Orgarn
200 g/4⅔ cups panko breadcrumbs
4 x chkn 'escalopes' (see page 13) or thick slices of 'chicken ham' (see page 14)
vegetable oil, for frying
a pinch of salt, to taste

SERVES 4

For the Japanese masala, lightly toast all the spices in a small frying pan/skillet over a low-medium heat. Mix well and set aside. Keep any excess in an airtight jar.

To make the curry roux, add the oil to a large frying pan/skillet and put over a medium heat. Add the flour and stir well. As it starts to cook, add the curry and chilli/chili powders. Cook gently for a few minutes, then add the remaining roux ingredients. Mix well until it makes a crumbly texture, then remove from the heat and set aside.

Heat the oil in a large pan on a medium–high heat. Add the onions and carrot and sauté for 20–30 minutes, stirring from time to time, until caramelized. Add the stock, banana, salt and curry powder and mix. Bring to a simmer and cook for a few minutes.

Add 1–2 ladlefuls of the onion stock to the roux and whisk together to make a thick, smooth paste. Add the smooth roux mixture back into the onion stock pan and mix well. Bring to a simmer and then using a stick blender, blitz the mixture until smooth. Season with salt to taste if needed. Keep warm.

To make the 'katsu', mix together the flour with the salt and pepper in a wide bowl. Mix up the vegan egg substitute into another bowl and place the panko on a large plate. Dip the chkn 'escalopes' or 'ham' slices into the flour and coat well. Then dip into the aquafaba or vegan egg and then into the panko breadcrumbs. Put on a baking sheet.

Heat the oil in a large, deep pan or wok to approximately 180°C/350°F. Put the escalopes into the oil and fry on each side for 3–4 minutes until crispy and golden. Remove and lay on paper towels.

To serve, slice the katsu into wide fingers and lay on top of the steamed rice. Pour over some of the curry sauce or serve with a small pot of sauce on the side. Try serving with a seaweed salad on the side.

THAI STUFFED 'OMELETTE'

Thai stuffed omelette is a classic street food, traditionally stuffed with minced pork. I decided to try a vegan version using a chickpea/gram flour batter and the results were utterly delicious and well worth sharing. Keep the batter mixture quite thin to make a more foldable pancake.

3 garlic cloves, finely chopped
1 heaped teaspoon coarsely ground black pepper
5-cm/2-inch trimmed roots from large bunch of fresh coriander/ cilantro, finely chopped
2 tablespoons vegetable oil, plus extra for the omelettes
1 banana shallot, thinly sliced
100 g/3½ oz. vegan mince
70 g/2½ oz. fine green beans, thinly sliced at an angle
handful of freshly chopped coriander/ cilantro leaves, to serve
soy sauce, to serve
hot pickled chillies/chiles, to serve

TO MAKE THE GRAM BATTER
85 g/½ cup chickpea/ gram flour
1 teaspoon baking powder
¼ teaspoon ground turmeric
large pinch of black salt
2 tablespoons soy sauce

MAKES 4 PARCELS

In a small bowl, whisk together the gram batter ingredients with 150 ml/⅔ cup water until smooth and then set aside for 5 minutes.

Using a pestle and mortar, mix together the garlic, black pepper and coriander/cilantro roots to form a paste. Place a large frying pan/skillet or wok on a medium heat and add 2 tablespoons vegetable oil and the shallot. Fry for 2–3 minutes until the shallot starts to soften and lightly brown. Then add the paste and cook for a few minutes. Add the mince and green beans and sauté over a medium heat for 4–5 minutes. Stir well and remove from the heat, then tip the contents onto a plate.

Add a little more oil to the frying pan/skillet, then pour in half the batter mixture and tilt the pan to make a thinner even layer. Cook briefly until the batter starts to set, then pile a quarter of the mince mixture (about 2 tablespoons) into the centre. Fold one side in, then turn and fold the next side in, and repeat folding in the other two sides gently to make a square package. Cook for a further few minutes until the batter is completely set. Place on a baking sheet in a low oven to keep warm while making the second one in the same way. Serve with a scattering of coriander/cilantro leaves, and some soy sauce and hot pickled chillies/chiles on the side.

FAUX FISH

There's a huge variety of faux fish and
seafood products in the freezer section
of large Chinese supermarkets. They can
make interesting additions to any faux fish
recipe although can be underwhelming
and a little rubbery on their own. Seaweeds
introduce great flavours from the sea
for vegan recipes and are also highly
nutritious. Another revelation for me
as a chef has been cooking with heart
of palm. It has a softer and very mild
artichoke-like flavour, and fascinating
structure adaptable to several easy dishes
with 'crab meat' and 'calamari'.

BURSTING BAGEL
WITH CARROT LOX & WATERCRESS RICOTTA

I think the idea of using slightly under-ripe vegetables as an alternative to smoked salmon is a very clever one. Slow roasting to bring out the sweetness, and then using smoky flavours to marinate the veg, makes a delicious substitute. A two-day marinade works best. Vegan cream cheese is readily available in major supermarkets now, but this watercress ricotta is nutritious and can be made in a larger batch, making it much more wallet-friendly.

FOR THE CARROT LOX
3 large carrots
450 g/1 lb. sea salt
1 tablespoon olive oil
2 teaspoons liquid smoke
½ teaspoon rice vinegar
  or apple cider vinegar

FOR THE WATERCRESS RICOTTA
300 g/2¼ cups whole
  blanched almonds
  (soak in water for an
  hour if they have skins,
  then rub off)
½ teaspoon acidophilus
  (optional)
small bunch of fresh
  watercress
1 small garlic clove, finely
  chopped
1 level teaspoon sea salt
½ teaspoon freshly
  ground black pepper
2 teaspoons freshly
  squeezed lemon juice

TO SERVE
2 vegan bagels, halved
2 tablespoons capers,
  drained
½ small red onion, thinly
  sliced
small handful of fresh dill
2–4 gherkins/pickles

SERVES 2–4

Preheat the oven to 190°C (375°F) Gas 5.

Top and tail the carrots, but do not peel. Wash the skins well and leave wet. Pour half the salt into a 500-g/18-oz. loaf pan. Lay the carrots on top, side by side. Cover with the remaining salt. Bake in the middle of the preheated oven for 1½ hours.

Remove from the oven, gently lift the carrots from the salt and leave to cool slightly. Brush off any excess salt, then, using your fingers, peel off the skin from the carrots. You can use a knife, but be careful not to peel away too much of the carrot flesh.

In a small deep dish, mix together the olive oil, liquid smoke and vinegar. Using a sharp knife or mandoline, slice the carrots into thin ribbons. Lay the carrot slices in the mixture, making sure they are well covered. Cover the bowl and put in the fridge overnight.

The next day, mix well again and massage slightly to rub in the flavours. Cover and leave overnight in the fridge.

The lox will be ready to use from the next day, and will keep for a further 5–6 days in the fridge. When ready to use, bring the lox to room temperature before serving.

To make the watercress ricotta, cover the blanched almonds in filtered water and soak overnight. The next day, drain and rinse the almonds, and blend until smooth with 235 ml/1 cup of filtered water and the acidophilus, if using. Place the mixture in a piece of muslin/cheesecloth, twist and place in a sieve/strainer over a pan. Leave to drain for 20 minutes.

Roughly chop the watercress, removing any very twiggy parts, and mix together in a small bowl with the garlic, salt, pepper and lemon juice. Leave to stand for 10–15 minutes. Add the ricotta and mix well. Tip back into the muslin/cheesecloth and twist tightly. Place back in the sieve/strainer over the pan, then leave in the fridge overnight to drain and set.

The next day, toast the bagel halves. Spread each half with the watercress ricotta and top with the carrot lox. Serve with the capers, red onion, a sprinkle of dill and a gherkin/pickle on the side, if you like.

CHIPPY-STYLE TOFISH
WITH CHIPS & TARTARE SAUCE

As a dish, fish and chips has twice won best dish in the British Street Food Awards during the last 5 years. It's a tough tradition to square up to with a vegan dish, but this tofish recipe is a tasty alternative and uses the same batter recipe that won Best of the Best at the BSFA 2015 (grateful thanks to my street food pal, Fish&'s Andrew Critchett, for this crispy deliciousness). For me, the secret is making sure the tofu has been frozen and defrosted again before use, to ensure a nice firm texture. You can fry the chips, of course, but I like to make baked skin-on wedges, which can be even tastier if dusted with a little garam masala or garlic powder.

FOR THE TOFISH
400-g/14-oz. block of firm tofu, excess water drained
1 teaspoon salt
1 sheet of nori seaweed
60 g/scant ½ cup plain/all-purpose flour
1 tablespoon cornflour/cornstarch
¼ teaspoon ground turmeric
120 ml/½ cup sparkling water

FOR THE TARTARE SAUCE
4 tablespoons vegan mayonnaise
1 tablespoon finely chopped fresh dill
½ tablespoon capers, drained and finely chopped
2 gherkins/pickles, finely diced

FOR THE CHIPS
5 large potatoes, scrubbed
2 tablespoons olive oil
1 teaspoon salt
1 teaspoon garam masala (optional)

approx. 480 ml/2 cups vegetable oil, for frying

SERVES 4

To make the tofish pieces, ensure the tofu block is completely defrosted. Place between the palms of your hands and press firmly but gently to ensure all the water is squeezed out. Slice the tofu lengthways through the middle, to make two large thinner slabs. Then slice each slab in two, slightly at an angle, to make an angular fish fillet shape. Cut the nori sheet into the same shape as the tofu 'fillets', and stick the slices of seaweed to one side of the tofu. Press down the nori and then lay the tofu on that side, to ensure that the seaweed stays in place. Season this side of the tofu 'fillets' with salt.

Prepare the tartare sauce by mixing together all the ingredients in a small bowl. Cover and set aside in the fridge.

Preheat the oven to 200°C (400°F) Gas 6. To make the chips, slice the potatoes lengthways to make wedges, as thin or thick as you like. Lay on a baking sheet and drizzle with the olive oil. Season with the salt and spice (if using). Using your hands, massage the wedges with the oil to ensure they are well coated and seasoned. Bake in the preheated oven for 20–25 minutes until crispy.

Put a heavy-based pan over a medium–high heat and half-fill with oil for frying. Heat to approx. 180°C/350°F.

Put the flour on a plate and coat the tofu pieces well. Set aside on greaseproof paper, nori-side down. Add the cornflour/cornstarch, salt and turmeric to the flour and mix with sparkling water to make a thin batter. Dip the tofu 'fillets' into the batter to coat, then gently put into the hot oil and deep-fry for 7–8 minutes, turning once, until golden and crispy. Try not to crowd the pan – it's better to fry the tofu in two batches and keep warm in a low oven. Drain on paper towels.

Serve the tofish with the chips and tartare sauce on the side. Garnish with lemon wedges and serve with chip shop-style mushy peas, if you like.

SHISO COURGETTE SCALLOPS
WITH TERIYAKI PINEAPPLE

I've come across a number of faux fish alternatives to scallops and other seafood. King oyster mushrooms can be trimmed and thickly sliced to make the stems look like scallops, especially when well seared. I've also cooked with vegan prawns/shrimps and scallop balls from the Chinese supermarket, but neither has won me over as much in terms of flavour without some additional ingredients. The key to using courgette/zucchini is to sear the pieces over a very high heat for a very short time.

4 pineapple rings, 1–2 cm/½–¾ inch thickness, cut into large pieces
2 large handfuls of seasonal baby salad leaves
2 medium-large firm courgettes/zucchini
1 tablespoon coconut oil
2 garlic cloves, crushed but not peeled

FOR THE TERIYAKI SAUCE
60 ml/¼ cup soy sauce
50 g/¼ cup unrefined brown sugar
2–3-cm/¾–1¼-inch piece of fresh ginger, peeled and finely chopped
2 garlic cloves, finely chopped
1 tablespoon agave syrup
1 teaspoon sesame oil
3 tablespoons mirin

FOR THE DRESSING
2 teaspoons sesame oil
1 tablespoon soy sauce
1 teaspoon rice vinegar
¼ teaspoon ground white pepper

TO SERVE
½ small red onion, very finely diced
seaweed mixed sprinkles, (optional)
handful of shiso leaves, roughly chopped (or use Thai basil)

SERVES 4

To make the teriyaki sauce, combine all the ingredients in a small pan and bring to the boil. Reduce the heat and simmer for 5 minutes. Remove from the heat and allow to cool. Once cooled, pour over the pineapple rings and leave to marinate for 20–30 minutes.

Prepare the dressing by mixing together all the ingredients in a bowl. Add the salad leaves and toss with your hands until well coated in the dressing.

Place a ridged griddle/grill pan on a high heat. Sear the pineapple slices for 4–5 minutes on each side until caramelized. Once cool, cut into pieces. Set aside.

To make the courgette/zucchini scallops, peel the courgettes/zucchini so that the skin is almost removed, but try to leave an almost translucent green thin layer. Slice into 2-cm/¾-inch slices, then trim the edges of each slice using the peeler, making a slight barrel shape.

Place a small frying pan/skillet over a medium heat and add the coconut oil. Add the garlic and fry for a few minutes to release the flavours into the oil. Remove the garlic from the oil, turn up the heat to max and fry the courgette/zucchini pieces for no more than 1 minute on each side. Remove from the pan and lay on paper towels to drain.

To serve, place the dressed salad leaves on a small plate then layer four courgette/zucchini pieces on top of the leaves. Place a few pieces of caramelized pineapple around the sides. Scatter the top with diced onion. Top with a generous spoonful of shiso or basil leaves. Serve immediately.

SAFFRON RAVIOLI
WITH HEART OF PALM & CHILLI

The pasta dough in this recipe uses aquafaba, or chickpea water, as an alternative to eggs. To reduce wastage, I often use just the centre part of heart of palm for this dish and save the outer part for making crispy calamari-style rings (see page 73). This makes a great Italian-inspired dinner, and will pleasantly surprise your seafood-loving friends.

FOR THE PASTA DOUGH
250 ml/1 cup plus
   1 tablespoon aquafaba
   (see page 12)
generous pinch of
   saffron threads
300 g/2¼ cups '00' flour,
   plus extra for dusting

FOR THE FILLING
½ x 410-g/14½-oz. can
   heart of palm, drained
   and chopped or use
   palm centres only
   using 1 can
1 tablespoon freshly
   chopped parsley
1 small garlic clove,
   finely chopped
2 tablespoons vegan
   cream cheese
½ teaspoon sea salt

TO SERVE
2–3 tablespoons good-
   quality olive oil
2 small garlic cloves,
   crushed but with skin
   left on
1–2 teaspoons dried chilli
   flakes/hot red pepper
   flakes
½–1 teaspoon fine sea
   salt, to taste

**MAKES APPROX. 12–16
LARGE RAVIOLI**

To make the dough, pour the aquafaba into a small pan, put over a high heat and bring to the boil. Add the saffron and simmer for 8–10 minutes until the liquid is reduced by at least a third. Set aside to cool. In a large bowl, add the flour and about 100 ml/⅓ cup plus 1 tablespoon of the aquafaba. Add up to another 50 ml/3½ tablespoons of the aquafaba. Using your hands, bring the dough together to make a firm but pliable dough. Knead for 5–10 minutes, and then cover with a damp cloth or clingfilm/plastic wrap and leave to rest for an hour or so at room temperature.

In a small bowl, add the heart of palm. Squeeze out any excess water and then mix in the parsley, garlic and the vegan cream cheese. Mix well and season with the salt. Set aside.

Divide the dough into 3 pieces. Roll out one piece to about 2–3 mm/⅛ inch thick (leave the other pieces covered so they don't dry out). Roll the dough out to approximately 40.5 x 25 cm/16 x 9¾ inches and slice in half lengthways, to make two large strips approximately 12.5 cm/5 inches wide.

Lay the pasta sheets on a lightly floured surface. Place 4 or 5 generous tablespoonfuls of the filling mixture in a line along each of the sheets. Brush the pasta around the filling with a little of the aquafaba, then lay another pasta sheet over the top and, using your hand, gently push out any air before sealing. Use a cookie cutter to cut out 4 or 5 circular pieces. Cover the pieces with a kitchen towel while you finish the remaining ravioli making 12–15 large pieces. The ravioli can be frozen at this stage (if you are not cooking them all) for up to 3 months, or they can be kept in the fridge for 2–3 days.

To cook the ravioli, put a large, deep pan over a high heat and half-fill with water. Bring to a rolling boil and then gently place the ravioli into the water. Bring back to the boil and reduce to a simmer, cooking for 5 minutes until the ravioli floats. Cook in batches, taking care not to overcrowd the pan. Carefully lift the ravioli out using a slotted spoon, and lay in a wide sieve/strainer on paper towels to drain.

In a small frying pan/skillet, add the olive oil and crushed garlic cloves. Fry over a medium-high heat for a minute or two, then add the chilli flakes/hot red pepper flakes and salt. Sauté for a further 2–3 minutes, then remove from the heat and discard the garlic. Put the ravioli pieces on a plate, drizzle over the chilli/chile oil and serve immediately.

SEA-LOVING SUSHI

This dish is inspired by some outstanding vegan sushi I had in San Fran and LA. I went back to see if it really was as good the second time, and it was.

FOR THE SUSHI RICE
100 g/generous ½ cup
   sushi rice
3 tablespoons sushi
   seasoning (rice
   vinegar, sugar and salt,
   if you want to make
   your own)
½ tablespoon mirin

FOR THE TOMATO LOX
4 firm vine tomatoes
2 tablespoons soy sauce
½ teaspoon liquid smoke
½ teaspoon caster/
   granulated sugar
1 teaspoon sesame oil
1 teaspoon olive oil

TO ASSEMBLE
chickpea chuna
   (see page 77)
1 lotus root, peeled and
   thinly sliced (in lemon
   water to prevent
   browning)
¼ cucumber, sliced in
   half lengthways and
   deseeded
6 sheets of nori seaweed,
   each cut in half
1 ripe avocado, peeled,
   pitted and cut into
   strips
1 teaspoon wasabi paste

approx. 250 ml/1 cup
   plus 1 tablespoon oil,
   for frying

MAKES ABOUT 20–25 PIECES

First prepare the rice. Rinse the rice in a sieve/strainer until the water runs clear. Put the rice in a pan with 120 ml/½ cup water. Leave for 30 minutes. Next, place the pan over a medium high heat, with the lid on. Bring to a simmer for 10 minutes, then remove from the heat. Leave the lid on to steam the rice for another 15 minutes. Fluff with a fork, then pour over the sushi seasoning and mirin. Stir well. Tip into a bowl and cover with a kitchen towel. Set aside.

To make the lox, half-fill a medium pan with water and bring to the boil. With a small paring knife, make a little cross on the bottom of each tomato. Drop the tomatoes into the boiling water and cook for a couple of minutes. Remove with a slotted spoon and drop in a bowl of iced water. Once cool, remove the skins. Carefully quarter the tomatoes then deseed, taking care to maintain the outer flesh part in one piece, like a large thick petal. Set aside.

Heat the oil for frying in a small pan. Gently fry the lotus root slices until just crisp. Drain on paper towels.

Slice the cucumber into long strips approximately 5 mm/¼ inch wide.

To prepare the sushi with tomato lox, lay out a sheet of clingfilm/plastic wrap. Then, using wet hands, lay some sushi rice on top, enough to cover approximately ½ a nori sheet, about

1 cm/⅜ inch thick. Then lay the ½ nori sheet on top and lay some avocado and cucumber strips down the centre. Using the clingfilm, roll the sushi firmly into a roll, so the vegetables are in the centre, wrapped in nori, then with the rice wrapping around outside of the seaweed. Uncover one side of the roll and layer on the tomato lox pieces. Lay the pieces closely adjacent, and covering one side of the roll. Wrap the clingfilm around the whole thing and twist the ends tightly. Repeat with one or two further rolls. Leave to set lin the fridge for about an hour. Each roll makes about 5 pieces.

To make the maki-style rolls, cut a sheet of the nori seaweed into strips. Roll a small amount of sushi rice in your hands then wrap the strip of nori around the rice ball, sealing with a couple of grains of rice as glue. The top will be open, and the rice should only fill about half the roll. Using your finger, rub a little wasabi onto the rice, pushing it down slightly, then add a generous spoonful of the chickpea chuna mixture on top. Repeat with the other strips, to make about 8–10 pieces.

To serve, slice the tomato sushi into 5 or 6 pieces per roll with a sharp knife, dipped in hot water. Place a crispy lotus root slice into the top of the maki rolls. Lay onto large platters to serve.

FAUX FISH PIE
WITH HERBY MASH

This hearty comfort dish brings together those familiar seafood pie flavours with some great vegan alternatives. I wanted to recreate the distinctive flaky, smoky and sweet flavours and have ramped up the flavours in the mash and the velvety sauce. You can substitute or leave out some of the faux fish alternatives if you find they are difficult to get hold of, but they are worth ordering online as most keep for months in the freezer.

2–3 tablespoons olive oil

3 banana shallots, finely chopped

1 carrot, finely diced

1 small leek, thinly sliced

2 tablespoons plain/all-purpose flour

300 ml/1¼ cups vegan milk

250 ml/1 cup plus 1 tablespoon good-quality vegetable stock

2 bay leaves

1 teaspoon smoked essence

10 g/⅓ oz. dried dulse seaweed, soaked in boiling water (I also use a dried seaweed mix)

1 x 410-g/14-oz. can heart of palm, drained and rinsed (or use artichoke hearts), roughly chopped

4 vegan 'prawns/shrimp', roughly sliced at an angle

2 vegan 'scallop' balls, roughly chopped into 1–2 cm/⅜–¾ inch pieces

100 g/3½ oz. fresh chard leaves, roughly chopped (or use spinach leaves)

large handful of freshly chopped dill

½–1 teaspoon sea salt

FOR THE HERBY MASH

6 large white potatoes, such as Maris Piper, peeled and quartered

4 tablespoons good-quality olive oil

60 ml/¼ cup vegan crème fraîche or cream

1–2 teaspoons fine sea salt, to taste

1 teaspoon ground white pepper

½ large bunch parsley, freshly chopped

80 g/scant 1 cup grated vegan cheese (optional)

large handful of fresh breadcrumbs (optional)

small handful of pumpkin seeds (optional)

wedge of lemon, to serve

SERVES 5–6

First, make the herby mash. Half-fill a large pan with water, cover and bring to the boil. Add the potatoes and boil for 20–30 minutes until completely soft. Drain into a colander and leave to drain and cool for 5–10 minutes. Put the potatoes back into the empty pan and add the olive oil. Mash vigorously, adding the crème fraîche or cream, salt and pepper, and whipping a little to make it smooth and creamy. Add the parsley and mix well. Set aside.

Preheat the oven to 180°C (350°F) Gas 4.

Put the olive oil into a deep frying pan/skillet, add the shallots and fry very gently, taking care not to colour them. Fry for 8–10 minutes until translucent and sticky. Add the carrot and leek, and fry for a further 6–7 minutes. Add the flour to the pan and mix well to make a chunky roux. Add the milk, mix well and continue to heat gently for a few minutes. Add the stock, bay leaves, smoked essence and seaweed to the pan, stirring well. Add all the remaining ingredients, season with the salt to taste, stir well and cook gently until the greens are wilted. Pour the mixture into a deep baking dish. Top with the herby mash, then sprinkle with the grated cheese, breadcrumbs and pumpkin seeds, if using.

Put the pie in the centre of the preheated oven, with a baking sheet underneath to catch any sauce bubbling over. Bake for 30–40 minutes until golden and crispy on top and the sides are bubbling.

Allow to stand for 5 minutes before serving with a wedge of lemon, if you like.

'FISH' FINGER DOORSTOP BUTTIES

I once asked John Torode, what is the best-selling dish in your restaurant (formerly Smiths of Smithfields, which had three floors ranging from an easy-going café on the ground floor to fine dining on top floor). Without missing a beat, he said it was the fish finger sandwich. I think my 'fish and chipocrite' husband would agree that this is the thing he misses the most on his mostly vegetarian diet. The heart of palm provides a nice flaky texture for the goujon and the homemade breadcrumbs are much more delicious than ready-made ones.

1 x 410-g/14-oz. can heart of palm, drained, rinsed and roughly chopped
½ teaspoon celery seeds
1 tablespoon celery leaves, finely chopped
¼ teaspoon finely chopped nori seaweed
½ teaspoon sea salt
1 teaspoon tapioca starch
2–3 slices of seeded bread
120 g/scant 1 cup plain/all-purpose flour
½ teaspoon sea salt
½ teaspoon ground white pepper
8 tablespoons aquafaba reduction (see page 12)
120 ml/½ cup olive oil, for shallow-frying

TO SERVE
4 thick slices of white bread
4 generous tablespoons tartare sauce (see page 57)
handful of rocket/arugula leaves

MAKES 5–6 FINGERS/SERVES 2

In a small bowl, mix together the chopped palm, celery seeds, leaves, seaweed, salt and tapioca starch. Set aside for 30 minutes.

Using a food processor, blitz the seeded bread to make a rough crumb. You can also use a hand grater to do this, on the largest tooth. Set aside on a small plate. On another plate, add the flour, salt and pepper, and mix well. Put the aquafaba into a shallow bowl.

Using your hands, take a small handful of the chopped palm mixture and shape into a small sausage or goujon shape. Dip into the flour and then into the aquafaba. Then roll in the breadcrumbs and lay on greaseproof paper ready for frying. Repeat with the remaining palm mixture to make five or six fingers. Cover the tray with clingfilm/plastic wrap and place in the fridge to set for an hour or so.

Put the olive oil into a large frying pan/skillet over a medium-high heat. Drop a breadcrumb in the oil and if it sizzles without burning the oil is ready. Gently lay half of the fingers into the hot oil and fry gently for 8–10 minutes, turning once. Once crispy and golden, drain on paper towels to remove any excess oil. You can keep the fingers warm and crispy in a low oven while you complete the next batch.

Butter the bread if you like, and slather one side of each slice generously with tartare sauce, lay half of the 'fish' fingers on top of two slices of bread and then some rocket/arugula leaves. Top each with another thick slice of buttered bread and serve.

TOGARASHI TACOS

These little tacos are a street food favourite on my corporate party menus. I have restaurant friends who shudder at the mention of the word 'fusion'. But togarashi spicing works well in the tempura for this baja-style taco. I order my corn tacos from an online supplier. You can buy them in small quantities and they come with a long shelf life. The chilli/chile dressing is one of my new favourites, with smoky ancho and tangy mango, it will keep for several weeks in the fridge.

FOR THE 'SLAW
¼ red cabbage, thinly sliced
¼ white cabbage, thinly sliced
2 tablespoons canned sweetcorn/corn kernels, drained and rinsed
freshly squeezed juice of 2 limes
1 tablespoon agave syrup or maple syrup
½ teaspoon sea salt
½ small red chilli/chile, finely chopped

FOR THE ANCHO CHILLI/CHILE & MANGO DRESSING
2 large dried ancho chillies/chiles, soaked in boiling water for 15 minutes, then drained
1 small ghost chilli/chile, soaked in boiling water for 15 minutes (or use 3–4 very hot bird's eye chillies/chiles), then drained
355 ml/1½ cups mango purée
1 teaspoon sea salt
1–2 tablespoons unrefined sugar or agave syrup

MAKES APPROX. 450 ML/ 15 FL. OZ. JAR

FOR THE FILLING
2 x 410-g/14-oz. cans heart of palm, drained and rinsed
150 g/1½ cups cornflour/cornstarch or potato starch
150 g/1 cup plus 2 tablespoons plain/all-purpose flour
1 teaspoon sea salt
2 teaspoons togarashi spice mix
200–300 ml/scant 1–1¼ cups sparkling water

TO ASSEMBLE
20 mixed blue and yellow corn tacos, 10 cm/4 inch width
6 tablespoons vegan mayonnaise
1 tablespoon pickled ginger strips
1 teaspoon black sesame seeds
approx. 450 ml/15 fl. oz. vegetable oil, for deep frying

SERVES 6

To make the 'slaw, mix together all the ingredients in a bowl. Set aside for 1 hour, longer if possible, to allow the cabbages to soften.

To make the dressing, add the chillies/chiles, 120 ml/½ cup water, the mango purée, salt and sugar or agave syrup to a pan. Bring to a simmer for 10 minutes, remove from the heat and purée using a stick blender. Taste the sauce and add more sugar and salt as needed. If too thick, add a little more water. Set aside at room temperature.

To make the filling, pat the heart of palm dry, then slice lengthways. Put the cornflour/cornstarch, flour, salt and togarashi spice mix into a large bowl. Add 200 ml/¾–1 cup of the water and whisk to make a loose batter. Add more water as needed, so the batter thinly coats the back of a spoon. Heat the oil in a large, deep pan to about 190°C/375°F. Test the temperature of the oil by dropping in a breadcrumb and if it sizzles without burning, the oil is ready.

Dip the heart of palm pieces into the batter to coat, shake gently to remove the excess then lay gently in the hot oil. Fry in batches for about 2–3 minutes on each side until the batter is crispy and golden. Drain on paper towels. Fry the remaining pieces, and set aside on a baking sheet in a low oven to keep warm.

Warm the tacos according to the packet instructions, then put two or three on each plate. Add a spoonful of the 'slaw mixture to each. Halve the fried palm pieces, then lay several pieces on top of each taco. Drizzle each with the mayo and some ancho chilli/chile & mango dressing, and top with ginger and sesame seeds if using. Serve immediately.

SESAME TOAST

When I was very young, I loved prawn/shrimp toast from the moment I crunched my way through that nutty sesame crust. I don't think it was ever about the prawns/shrimp to be honest, and I would encourage even the biggest seafood lover to give this recipe a try – if for no other reason than to take a little pressure off the mangrove-sapping prawn/shrimp farms of South East Asia. I suppose you might say it's just pimped-up fried bread, but let's face it, what's not to like about fried bread! Well-made fried bread is a dangerous treat indeed with its moreish carby crunch and dastardly calorie content. But everything in moderation, so this little treat makes a great starter or side dish for a Chinese-inspired dinner. Serve with some dipping pots of light soy and sweet chilli/chili sauces.

1 tablespoon soy sauce
1.5 cm/½-inch piece of fresh ginger, finely minced (or use 1 teaspoon ginger paste)
1 heaped tablespoon cornflour/cornstarch
6 tablespoons aquafaba (see page 12), or use vegan 'egg' substitute such as Orgran
1 spring onion/scallion, thinly sliced
5-cm/2-inch piece of courgette/zucchini, finely chopped
2 mushrooms, finely chopped

2 vegan 'prawns/shrimp', finely chopped (optional)
3 slices of white bread, crusts removed
2 teaspoons sesame seeds
approx. 300 ml/1¼ cups vegetable oil, for deep-frying
sweet chilli/chili sauce, to serve

SERVES 2–4

Put the soy sauce in a bowl, then add the ginger and cornflour/cornstarch and mix to a paste. Whisk the aquafaba or egg substitute until fluffy and add to the soy mixture.

Add the chopped vegetables and vegan 'prawn/shrimp' (if using) to the soy mixture, and mix well to make a thick porridge-like paste. Lay the bread on a board, and then cover the top of each with about one third the mixture, ensuring the bread is well covered with the vegetables and paste. Using the palm of your hand, firmly press the mixture into the bread. Sprinkle a generous layer of sesame seeds over the top, gently pressing onto the vegetable mixture.

Heat approximately 5 cm/2 inches of oil in a deep frying pan/skillet or wok until approximately 190°C/375°F. Check the temperature by adding a crumb of bread. It should float to the top and sizzle immediately. Carefully lift the covered bread and gently place in the hot oil. Using a spatula, make sure the oil covers the bread so it cooks on both sides. Once the vegetable mixture has started to set, you can carefully turn the bread over if needed. Fry until the bread and sesame top turns golden brown, for approximately 5–6 minutes.

Remove from the pan with some tongs, and place on paper towels to drain off the excess oil. Cut into quarters and serve with sweet chilli/chili sauce. If you are making a larger batch, place the cooked pieces in a low oven to keep warm and crispy until ready to serve.

HEART OF PALM 'CALAMARI'
WITH GARLIC AIOLI

This recipe has appeared elsewhere within other much longer recipes as an optional addition. Hardly fair for a recipe that makes an impressive appetizer or sharing plate! You can flavour the batter with whatever spicing you like. I favour Korean red pepper flakes, but you can also keep this plain and simple served with nothing more than lemon wedges.

FOR THE 'CALAMARI' RINGS
200 g/7 oz. heart of palm 'rings'
1 tablespoon rice flour
1 tablespoon potato flour
1 tablespoon plain/all-purpose flour
½ teaspoon sea salt
2 tablespoons Korean pepper flakes or powder
150–250 ml/1 cup plus 1 tablespoon sparkling water
300–400 ml/1¼–scant 1¾ cups vegetable oil, for deep frying, such as sunflower or rapeseed oil

FOR THE AIOLI
6 tablespoons vegan mayonnaise
½ tablespoon freshly squeezed lemon juice
1 small garlic clove, finely chopped
¼ teaspoon sea salt
¼ teaspoon ground white pepper

SERVES 3–4

To make the aioli, mix together all the ingredients in a small bowl. Set aside.

To make the 'calamari' rings, rinse the heart of palm stems and drain on paper towels. Slice into 2.5-cm/1-inch rounds. Carefully push out the centre of each ring with your fingertip (this flaky part of the palm is perfect for making the ravioli filling on page 61). Repeat with the other rounds.

Mix the rice, potato and plain/all-purpose flour together in a small bowl, add the salt and Korean pepper powder. Add 150 ml/⅔ cup of the sparkling water and mix well to form a runny batter that should coat the back of a spoon. Add more sparkling water, if needed.

Heat the oil for frying in a small frying pan/skillet until approximately 190°C/375°F. Check the oil temperature with a small drop of batter, it should sizzle but not burn. Dip the rings into the batter to coat and then carefully drop into the hot oil, frying in batches of 6 or 7 for 2–3 minutes until the batter is golden and crispy. Drain on paper towels. Serve immediately with lemon wedges and the aioli dip.

LOBSTA ROLLS
WITH SMOKY PEPPER 'BISQUE'

A simple and flavoursome recipe using heart of palm, recreating some of the flavours of this New England favourite. You could also substitute some of the vegan fish alternatives (including faux lobster) available in the Chinese supermarket, although I find they can lack the tenderness of real seafood, so heart of palm works exceptionally well as an alternative here. Artichoke hearts also make a great seasonal alternative and are easy to buy in jars. Of course the bisque isn't really a bisque, with its rich seafood umami from roasted and simmered shells. I'm not sure anything vegan will ever taste like that.

1 x 410-g/14-oz. can heart of palm, drained and rinsed, or substitute 1 jar of artichoke hearts, drained

80 g/generous ⅓ cup vegan mayonnaise

2 teaspoons freshly squeezed lemon juice

65 g/2½ oz. chopped celery, including leaves and tender inner sticks/stalks

1 tablespoon freshly chopped parsley

½ teaspoon celery seeds

2 spring onions/scallions, finely chopped

1 teaspoon dried mixed seaweed or use nori seaweed, very finely chopped

½ tablespoon sriracha or other chilli/chili sauce

¼ teaspoon fine sea salt

¼ teaspoon ground white pepper

FOR THE 'BISQUE'

3 large red (bell) peppers, halved, deseeded and core removed

¼ fennel head

1 onion, unpeeled and quartered

1 large carrot, chopped

2 garlic cloves, unpeeled

400 ml/1¾ cups good quality vegetable stock

2 bay leaves

2 tablespoons vegan crème fraîche or soured/sour cream

2 teaspoons smoked paprika

1½ tablespoons tomato purée/paste

1 teaspoon ground coriander

1 teaspoon sea salt

TO SERVE

4 vegan hotdog rolls

2 tablespoons coconut butter or vegan margarine, gently melted

¼ iceberg lettuce, thinly sliced

1–2 tablespoons vegan soured/sour cream, to serve (optional)

SERVES 4

Roughly chop the palm stems. You want a mixture of the flaky middle parts and larger chunks of the outer stems. In a separate bowl, combine the mayo, lemon juice, celery, parsley, celery seeds, spring onions/scallions, seaweed, sriracha, salt and pepper. Mix well and set aside for 10 minutes, then taste and adjust the seasoning as necessary.

Preheat the oven to 200°C (400°F) Gas 6. To make the bisque, put the (bell) peppers, fennel, onion and carrot on a lightly oiled baking sheet. Roast in the preheated oven for 10–15 minutes and then add the garlic cloves. Roast for another 10–15 minutes, until the veggies are all well caramelized, then remove the baking sheet and set aside to cool. Remove the skin from the onion and garlic, and discard.

Add the roasted vegetables to a medium-sized pan along with the stock, tomato purée/paste, coriander and bay leaves. Bring to the boil and simmer for 10–15 minutes. Remove the bay leaves. Using a stick blender or food processor, blitz the mixture to make a smooth soup. Stir in the crème fraîche or soured/sour cream and salt and mix well.

Slice the hotdog rolls almost in half along the top, and brush the insides generously with the coconut butter or margarine. Lightly toast the rolls by placing on a hot dry frying pan/skillet or under a hot grill/broiler if you like. Half-fill each roll with lettuce and then add 2–3 tablespoons of the lobsta mixture.

To serve, divide the soup between four small cups or bowls (drizzle with a little vegan soured/sour cream) and serve alongside the lobsta rolls.

CHICKPEA CHUNA QUESADILLAS
WITH JICAMA SLAW

This is a very quick and easy dish to prepare, and super healthy too. I first came across canned toona in a vegan mall in Portland (my favourite vegan haven in the beautiful Pacific Northwest). It was a revelation, if only regarding the wide availability of specifically faux produce across the US. I bought some faux jerky too, but this definitely wasn't something I was planning to recreate anytime soon. Maybe it's a cultural thing and gets lost in translation.

FOR THE CHICKPEA CHUNA
1 x 400-g/14-oz. can of chickpeas, drained and rinsed
4 tablespoons finely diced celery, including chopped leaves
½ red onion, finely diced
3 tablespoons hummus or vegan mayonnaise
freshly squeezed juice of ½ lemon
½ teaspoon garlic powder
¼ teaspoon chilli/chili powder
½ teaspoon sea salt
½ teaspoon ground white pepper
⅛ sheet of nori seaweed, blitzed or chopped to a fine crumb

FOR THE JICAMA SLAW
200 g/7 oz. jicama, peeled
¼ cucumber, halved lengthways and deseeded
1 carrot, peeled
2 tablespoons rice vinegar
1 tablespoon freshly squeezed lime juice
large pinch of sea salt

4 large flour tortillas
ancho chilli/chile & mango dressing (see page 69) or use any other chilli/chili sauce (optional)

SERVES 2–4

To make the jicama slaw, slice the vegetables into thin 2.5 cm/1 inch matchsticks. Mix the vegetables together with the remaining ingredients in a small bowl. Set aside for 10 minutes.

To make the chickpea chuna, mash the chickpeas with a fork in a small bowl. Add all the remaining ingredients and mix well. Set aside.

Put a large frying pan/skillet over a medium-high heat, and put a large tortilla in the pan. Add 2–3 generous tablespoons of the chickpea mixture into the centre and fold the tortilla in half, pressing down slightly to spread the mixture out inside but without spilling out of the edges.

Toast for a minute or two, then carefully turn over and toast on the second side for another minute. Slide the quesadilla onto a chopping board and slice in half to serve. Repeat with the remaining tortillas and chickpea mixture. Serve two pieces per portion with a heap of jicama slaw on top, and drizzle with the chilli/chili dressing or sauce, if you like.

FAST
FOOD
FIXES

As a long-term veggie, I've never been a massive fan of fast food. For the longest time the plant-based options have been so limited. But times have changed and fast food menus are finally catching up with our American cousins with vegan 'chicken' shops, burger joints and diners popping up all over the UK. These recipes for plant-based meaty alternatives are packed with great flavour and texture, and give fast food satisfaction with real bite.

HELL YEAH CHILLI DOGS
PAPRIKA SEITAN 'DOGS' WITH GREEN JACKFRUIT & 3 BEAN CHILLI & NACHO CHEESE

This vegan hotdog can be eaten any which way you prefer. Plain and simple with some fried onions, mustard and ketchup, or it can be 'dressed up to the nines' with all your favourite toppings. The components of this recipe can also be used for lots of other dishes, especially the jackfruit chilli (see page 126).

FOR THE PAPRIKA SEITAN 'DOGS'
150 g/5½ oz. vital wheat gluten flour
2 tablespoons nutritional yeast
2 tablespoons chickpea/gram flour
1 tablespoon ground flaxseeds/linseeds
1 small onion, finely chopped
½ carrot, finely chopped
3 garlic cloves, crushed and chopped
2 tablespoons soy sauce
1 tablespoon tomato purée/paste
2 teaspoons smoked paprika
1 teaspoon ground coriander
1 teaspoon ground mustard seeds
½ teaspoon ground white pepper
½ teaspoon freshly ground black pepper
½ teaspoon celery seeds
pinch of ground nutmeg
1 teaspoon hickory liquid smoke
1 teaspoon smoked salt

FOR THE NACHO CHEESE
60 g/½ cup cashews
1½ teaspoons white miso paste
3 tablespoons tapioca starch
3 tablespoons nutritional yeast
1½ teaspoons freshly squeezed lemon juice
1 teaspoon paprika
1 teaspoon agave syrup or maple syrup
1 teaspoon onion powder
½ teaspoon ground turmeric
½ teaspoon garlic powder

TO SERVE
8 hotdog rolls, sliced lengthways
200 g/7 oz. green jackfruit & 3 bean chilli (see page 126)
nacho corn chips
pickled red chillies/chiles, roughly chopped
½ small red onion, finely diced

8 x squares of greaseproof paper

SERVES 8

To start the nacho cheese, soak the cashews in cold water for 3–4 hours, or overnight.

To make the paprika seitan 'dogs', mix together the vital wheat gluten, nutritional yeast, chickpea/gram flour and flaxseeds/linseeds in a large bowl, making a well in the centre. Place the remaining ingredients into a food processor and blitz to make a purée. Add 1–2 tablespoons of water if the mixture is too thick. Pour the liquid into the centre of the well and, with gloved hands, bring the mixture together to make a firm dough. If the dough seems too stiff, add another 1–2 tablespoons of water.

Divide the dough into eight equal pieces and roll each piece into a sausage shape. Put a greaseproof square on the work surface and put a sausage inside. Roll the sausage again on the surface, wrapping it in the paper. Twist the ends closed, then cover with a foil square. Repeat for all the sausages. Set a basket steamer over a pan of hot water, put the 'dogs' inside, cover with a lid and steam for 45 minutes. Set aside to cool in the wrappers. The 'dogs' can be kept in the fridge for up to a week or in the freezer for a month.

To finish the nacho cheese, drain the cashews and rinse well. Put the cashews and remaining ingredients into a blender with 240 ml/1 cup water and blitz until smooth. Pour into a small pan over a medium heat. Whisk gently and bring to a simmer. Heat for a few minutes and the sauce will become gooey and glossy.

To serve, reheat the 'dog' by simmering in water for 2 minutes. Put a 'dog' inside each roll, ladle over some jackfruit chilli, crumble the nacho chips over the top, drizzle over the nacho cheese, and finish with pickled red chillies/chiles and onion.

EMPANADAS
WITH CHIMICHURRI SAUCE

Empanadas are adaptable to all kinds of fillings, both savoury and sweet. The traditional Argentinian-style or 'mendocinas' are filled with beef picadillo, a smoky spicy mix spiked with green olives. The potent flavour combination works well with the seitan mince to create a flavourful little stuffed pastry. Easy to freeze and make great picnic or party food.

FOR THE PASTRY
500 g/3¾ cups plain/all-purpose '00' flour, plus extra for dusting
2 teaspoons baking powder
½ teaspoon sea salt
160 g/5½ oz. Trex or vegan margarine, finely chopped
2–3 tablespoons vegan milk

FOR THE FILLING
2 tablespoons coconut oil
1 large onion, finely chopped
3 garlic cloves, finely chopped
1 red (bell) pepper, deseeded and chopped into 6 mm/¼ inch dice
2 spring onions/scallions, thinly sliced
2 teaspoons paprika
¼–½ teaspoon chilli/chili powder
1½ teaspoons ground cumin
1 teaspoon dried oregano
350 g/12 oz. seitan mince, or substitute 500 g/18 oz. oyster mushrooms, roughly chopped
1 tablespoons tomato purée/paste
25 g/1 oz. pitted green olives, roughly chopped
½–1 teaspoon salt, to taste

FOR THE CHIMICHURRI SAUCE
1 medium bunch of fresh Italian parsley
1 medium bunch of fresh oregano leaves
4 garlic cloves, peeled
60 ml/¼ cup red wine vinegar
1 teaspoon Korean red pepper flakes, or ½ teaspoon chilli/hot red pepper flakes
1 teaspoon salt
½ teaspoon freshly ground black pepper
120 ml/½ cup good-quality olive oil

2–3 tablespoons vegan milk, for brushing
1 teaspoon nigella seeds

pastry cutter
lightly oiled baking sheet

MAKES ABOUT 20 MEDIUM OR 30 SMALL EMPANADAS

To make the pastry, put the flour, baking powder and salt in a large bowl. Add the margarine, then, using your fingertips, rub the mixture together until it resembles breadcrumbs. Add the milk and mix to bring the dough together. Wrap in clingfilm/plastic wrap or cover in a bowl. Refrigerate for 45 minutes.

To make the filling, put the coconut oil in a large, deep frying pan/skillet over a medium-high heat. Add the onion and fry for 10–12 minutes until well softened. Add the garlic and cook for 2–3 minutes. Then add the (bell) pepper, the white parts of the spring onions/scallions, paprika, chilli/chili powder, cumin and oregano. Fry gently for 4–5 minutes. Add the seitan mince (or mushrooms if using) and tomato purée/paste and cook gently for 6–7 minutes, stirring well. Remove from the heat and add the olives and the green parts of the spring onions/scallions. Mix well, add salt to taste and set aside to cool.

Preheat the oven to 180°C (350°F) Gas 4 .

On a well-floured surface, roll out the dough to 3–4 mm/⅛ inch thickness, and using the pastry cutter, cut out small (10-cm/4-inch) or medium (14-cm/5½-inch) discs. Place a pastry disc in one hand, brush the edges with milk and add 1–2 tablespoons of the filling. Fold over the pastry to make a half-moon shape. Seal the edges using a fork to press together. Repeat with the other pastry discs. Lay the empanadas on the oiled baking sheet and brush the tops lightly with vegan milk. Sprinkle with nigella seeds. Bake in the middle of the preheated oven for 20–25 minutes until the pastry is golden.

To make the chimichurri sauce, put all of the ingredients into a blender and blitz for a few minutes. Serve the empanadas with the sauce on the side.

CLUB SANDWICH
CHKN, RASHER & AVOCADO

This recipe makes a simple large mock chicken roast, which can then be sliced. This roast is delicious with stuffing and all the traditional accompaniments for a Sunday dinner too.

FOR THE BRAISING STOCK
2 litres/2 quarts good-quality vegetable stock
1 large thumb-sized piece of fresh ginger, peeled and finely sliced
1 sheet of kombu seaweed, broken into pieces and soaked in cold water for 20 minutes, then drained
4 dried mushrooms, such as porcini or shiitake
120 ml/½ cup soy sauce

FOR THE CHKN ROAST
350 g/12 oz. vital wheat gluten flour
3 tablespoons chickpea/gram flour
2 tablespoons flavourless coconut or vegetable oil
1 leek, washed and finely chopped
4 garlic cloves, chopped
6 spring onions/scallions, thinly sliced
2 teaspoons salt
2 tablespoons soy sauce
2 teaspoons onion powder
1 teaspoon garlic powder
3 teaspoons ground coriander
1 tablespoon brown miso paste
1½ teaspoons dried mixed herbs

FOR THE SPICE RUB
1 tablespoon dried mixed herbs
½ tablespoon ground white pepper
½ tablespoon freshly ground black pepper
1 teaspoon salt

TO SERVE
2 tablespoons flavourless coconut or vegetable oil
4–6 mock smoky bacon rashers (page 12) or use ready-made
5–6 generous tablespoons vegan mayonnaise
1 tablespoon freshly squeezed lemon juice
2 garlic cloves, finely minced
4 thick slices from a sourdough boule/pain de campagne
1 ripe avocado, peeled, pitted and lightly mashed with
1 tablespoon freshly squeezed lime juice
a large handful of baby rocket/arugula leaves

well-oiled muslin/cheesecloth
twine

SERVES 2

To make the braising stock, put all of the ingredients into a large pan and simmer over a medium heat for 20 minutes. Remove from the heat and set aside.

For the chkn roast, put the wheat gluten and chickpea/gram flours into a large bowl. Mix well and set aside. Put the oil into a large frying pan/skillet and put over a medium heat. Add the leek, garlic and spring onions/scallions, then fry gently for 7–8 minutes until the vegetables are softened. Add the salt, soy sauce, onion, garlic powder, miso paste, mixed herbs and ground coriander. Mix well, then remove from the heat and add the mixture to the flour bowl. Add a little of the braising stock to the flour mixture, a few tablespoons at a time, and mix well to make a firm dough. Set aside for 20 minutes.

Preheat the oven to 180°C (350°F) Gas 4.

Mix the spice rub ingredients together and scatter on a clean work surface. Shape the dough into a large, thick roll, approximately 8 x 25 cm (3¼ x 9¾ inches). Roll in the dry spice mix so the outside is evenly coated. Then place at one end of a well-oiled muslin/cheesecloth, and roll firmly to ensure a snug fit. Twist the ends and secure with twine. Put the roll into a large, deep baking pan and pour over the remaining stock. Cover with foil and bake in the oven for 2 hours. Remove the roast from the pan and set aside still wrapped for 20–30 minutes.

In a small frying pan/skillet, add the oil and put over a high heat. Add the rashers and fry quickly to brown slightly. Remove and set aside. In a small bowl, mix together the mayo, lemon juice and garlic. Toast the sourdough, then spread the bottom slices with avo mash, add a couple of slices of the chkn roll, and top with rocket/arugula, then a couple of rashers. Drizzle with the mayo, and top each with another toasted slice of sourdough.

BABY GOT NO BEEF BURRITO
WITH CHARRED CORN SALSA & GREEN RICE

I make these burritos regularly at home, and not least because they are a spin-off recipe from my jackfruit chilli (which I often stretch to three different meals by batch cooking). Burritos are easy to make and probably one of the more nutritious fast foods, especially when filled with all this delicious plant-based goodness. Shortcuts are totally possible – leftover plain rice instead of green rice, or any chopped salad or even no salad instead of charred corn salsa. And make an extra one for lunch the next day!

FOR THE SALSA
2 red pointed (bell) peppers
400 g/scant 3 cups frozen sweetcorn/corn kernels, defrosted or use fresh cobs/ears if in season
1 jalapeño or hot green chilli/chile, diced
½ red onion, diced
handful of fresh coriander/cilantro leaves, plus extra to serve
1 teaspoon salt
freshly squeezed juice of 1 lime

FOR THE GREEN RICE
large bunch of fresh coriander/cilantro
small handful of fresh mint
1–2 teaspoons salt, to taste
4 garlic cloves, peeled
120 g/⅔ cup basmati rice

TO SERVE

4 large flour tortillas, 30 cm/12 inches in diameter
240 g/8½ oz. green jackfruit & 3 bean chilli (see page 126)
vegan soured/sour cream, such as Oatly Crème Fraîche
pickled red chillies/chiles (optional)
hot sauce (optional)

lightly oiled baking sheet

SERVES 4

To make the salsa, roast the (bell) peppers over an open flame or under a very hot grill/broiler until blackened all over. Put in a bowl, cover and set aside for a few minutes. Meanwhile, put the sweetcorn/corn kernels on a lightly oiled baking sheet. Put under a very hot grill/broiler for about 12–14 minutes until the corn has blackened slightly. Turn as needed. Set aside to cool slightly. If using fresh corn cobs/ears, preheat the oven to 220°C (425°F) Gas 7. Wrap the cobs in foil with a little olive oil and salt, then roast in the oven for 30–40 minutes. Put the remaining salsa ingredients into a small bowl and mix well. Peel, deseed and roughly dice the roasted (bell) peppers and add to the bowl along with the charred corn. Mix the salsa well and set aside in the fridge.

To make the green rice, blend all the ingredients, apart from the rice, with 175 ml/¾ cup water. Put the rice in a steamer or pan and pour over the green blended liquid. Steam or cook over a low heat until the rice is al dente. If using a pan, cook until al dente, then cover the pan with a clean kitchen towel and lid, and set aside to steam for 10–15 minutes. Fluff the rice well with a fork before serving.

To assemble, warm the tortillas on a plate covered with a damp paper towel in the microwave on High for about 40 seconds. Lay a tortilla on a flat surface. Place 2 heaped tablespoons of green rice across the centre, then 2 tablespoons of jackfruit chilli and 2 tablespoons of salsa. Add the sliced avocado, if using. Finally, layer a dollop of sour/soured cream and a sprinkle of pickled chillies/chiles or hot sauce if you like. Roll up, then slice in half to serve.

TORTA AHOGADA
MEXICAN CHILLI SAUSAGE SUB

When I first spied Torta Ahogada, I thought it rather incongruous to be selling cake from a San Diego taco truck. Until I realised this Mexican torta is in fact an enormous sausage sandwich (rather than a European-style tart or cake). Bearing a strong resemblance to the American-style sub, 'ahogada' refers to the 'drowning' of the entire roll in chilli/chili sauce. This seitan-based sausage recipe is spiced with chipotle in adobo sauce and ancho chilli/chili powder, ingredients you may need to source online. You could also substitute the sausage with a ready-made vegan chorizo, if you like. I use bird's-eye Thai chillies/chiles in the sauce rather than chiles de arbol, their Mexican counterpart. Freeze any extra sausages and try serving them chopped up in a breakfast burrito with fried potatoes, (bell) peppers and onions (nacho cheese, see page 80, in the centre turns this burrito twist into a winning dinner, too).

FOR THE SPICY SAUSAGE
3 tablespoons flavourless coconut oil or vegetable oil
1 red onion, finely chopped
6 garlic cloves, finely chopped
½ 200-g/7-oz. can chipotle chillies/chiles in adobo sauce (approx. 110 g/3¾ oz.)
1 teaspoon ancho chilli/chili powder (optional)
1 teaspoon smoked paprika
1 teaspoon ground cumin
1 teaspoon chilli/chili powder
1 teaspoon garlic powder

FOR THE WET MIX
120 g/generous ¾ cup canned white beans (such as cannellini)
200 ml/generous ¾ cup vegetable stock
80 ml/⅓ cup aquafaba (from the canned beans, see page 12)
2 tablespoons soy sauce
1 tablespoon mesquite liquid smoke
1 tablespoon maple syrup or agave syrup
1 tablespoon chilli/chile oil

FOR THE DRY MIX
150 g/5½ oz. vital wheat gluten flour
2 tablespoons nutritional yeast
2 tablespoons chickpea/gram flour
1 teaspoon dried oregano

To make the spicy sausage, put the coconut or vegetable oil into a frying pan/skillet and place over a medium heat. Add the onion and fry gently for 8–10 minutes until translucent. Add the garlic and chipotle adobo, along with the ancho powder, paprika, cumin, chilli/chili powder and garlic powder. Fry gently for 5 minutes, then set aside to cool a little. Tip the cooled mixture onto a board and roughly chop.

Using a stick blender or food processor, blitz together all the wet mix ingredients to make a smooth paste. Pour into a bowl and then add the onion-chilli/chile mixture and mix well.

In a large bowl, mix together the dry mix ingredients. Using gloved hands, make a well in the dry mix, then add the wet onion mix, making sure to combine well. Add a little water if needed, a tablespoon or two at a time, so the dough is not too dry. Knead the dough firmly for 3–4 minutes. You can also use a mixer with a dough hook. Divide the dough into four equal parts and roll them into sausage shapes.

Place each sausage onto a waxed paper square, pointing corner to corner. Roll the sausage trying to ensure an even shape along the length, fold in the ends and wrap the paper tightly. Then repeat with a foil square, wrapping so it is firmly wrapped. Place the sausages on a steamer tray inside a large, wide pan with a lid. Bring the water to the boil and steam

FOR THE HOT SAUCE

3 tablespoons pumpkin seeds/pepitas
1 tablespoon sesame seeds
60–100 ml/¼–⅓ cup vegetable stock
½ teaspoon ground allspice
1 tablespoon dried oregano
1 tablespoon ground cumin
4 bird's-eye red chillies/chiles, dried or fresh
1 tablespoon sea salt
3 garlic cloves, peeled
160 ml/generous ⅔ cup apple cider vinegar
1 tablespoon habanero hot sauce
1 x 400-g/14-oz. can plum tomatoes

TO SERVE

4 crusty sub-style rolls
3–4 tablespoons vegan feta or ricotta, crumbled
1 small red onion, thinly sliced
handful of freshly chopped coriander/cilantro
freshly squeezed juice of 1 lime

4 x lightly oiled squares of waxed paper, approx. 20 cm/8 inches square
4 x squares of foil, approx. 20 cm/8 inches square

SERVES 4 / MAKES 4 LARGE SAUSAGES

the sausages for 1 hour. Alternatively, to oven bake, preheat the oven to 180°C (350°F) Gas 4. Put 2 litres/2 quarts plus ½ cup of vegetable stock into a deep baking pan and place in the oven. Add the sausages and braise in the preheated oven for 1 hour.

Once cooked, leave to cool (still wrapped), then leave in the fridge for at least 1 hour, overnight if possible, to firm up. The next day, remove the wrappings and the sausages are ready to use.

Preheat the oven to 180°C (350°F) Gas 4.

To make the hot sauce, scatter the pumpkin and sesame seeds on a dry baking sheet and toast in the preheated oven for 10 minutes. Blend together half of the stock with all of the remaining sauce ingredients and 360 ml/1½ cups water, adding the toasted seeds and blitzing well to make a thick dressing. Add more of the vegetable stock as needed to make a thick but pourable sauce.

Slice the sausages lengthways and place on a hot griddle/grill pan, searing well for a few minutes on each side, then transfer to a plate. Slice the sub rolls lengthways and brush generously with the hot sauce, then place on the hot griddle/grill pan. Toast for a few minutes, then put onto plates. Top the rolls with the sausages, crumbled vegan feta or ricotta, onion, coriander/cilantro and a splash of lime juice if you like. Drizzle all over with more hot sauce and serve with napkins!

FIERY FLATBREAD PIZZAS
WITH BLACKENED SPICY SAUSAGE, SQUASH PUREE & CRISPY CAVOLO NERO

This pizza-like flatbread has a delicious combination of flavours and textures that I defy even the most committed of pepperoni pizza lovers not to fall in love with. It makes great sharing food too. The smoky and spicy sausage is also great on the BBQ for a Mexican- inspired hotdog. And the squash purée makes a delicious dip or canapé topping. I sometimes use aubergine/eggplant instead of squash for a change, which can be roasted whole then mashed with a fork.

FOR THE DOUGH
½ teaspoon fast-acting dried yeast
1 teaspoon caster/granulated sugar
280 ml/scant 1¼ cups lukewarm water
330 g/2⅓ cups strong white bread flour, plus extra for dusting
1 tablespoon olive oil
1 teaspoon salt

FOR THE TOPPINGS
1 butternut squash, peeled and cored
6 tablespoons olive oil
1 red onion, thinly sliced
2 small banana shallots, finely diced
4 garlic cloves, finely diced
1 tablespoon freshly chopped thyme (or 1 teaspoon dried)
100 ml/⅓ cup Marsala wine or sweet sherry
120 ml/½ cup good-quality vegetable stock

1 teaspoon salt
½ teaspoon freshly ground black pepper
1 teaspoon agave syrup
1 small bunch of cavolo nero (or use curly kale or other dark winter greens)
2 Mexican spicy chilli sausages (see page 88), cut into 1–2-cm/⅜-inch slices (or substitute any vegan chorizo)

polenta/cornmeal, for dusting
2–3 tablespoons almond 'ricotta' or other vegan alternative
2 tablespoons pumpkin seeds/pepitas, lightly toasted
chilli/chile oil, to drizzle (optional)
vegan 'Parmesan' hard style cheese (optional)

SERVES 4

First, make the dough. Mix the yeast, sugar and water together in a small bowl. Stir well and set aside in a warm place for 10–20 minutes until nice and frothy. If it doesn't froth, start again. I use a mixer to start this pizza-like dough, but it can be made equally well using your hands. Put the flour, oil and salt into a large bowl, add the liquid and mix well. Knead until the dough is smooth and no longer sticky, usually about 10 minutes of kneading or mixing.

Turn the dough out onto a well-floured surface and knead well for a further 10 minutes. Continue until the dough is very stretchy and springy. Place the dough in a well-oiled bowl and cover. Leave in a warm place for 30 minutes until doubled in size. Divide the dough into four large balls. Cover and set aside.

Preheat the oven to 200°C (400°F) Gas 6.

Cut the butternut squash into large pieces and put onto a lightly oiled baking sheet. Bake in the preheated oven for 20–30 minutes until the pieces are well softened and starting to blacken at the edges. Remove from the oven and set aside. Reduce the oven temperature to 140°C (275°F) Gas 1.

In a small frying pan/skillet, add 2 tablespoons of the olive oil and the red onion. Fry over a medium high heat for about 5–6 minutes until browned. Set aside on a small plate to cool.

In the same frying pan/skillet, add the shallots and a further 2 tablespoons of olive oil. Fry the shallots over a low heat until softened and translucent, then add the garlic and cook for a further 3–4 minutes.

Add the thyme, wine or sherry (if using), stock, salt, pepper and agave syrup. Mix well and bring to a simmer, cooking for about 3–4 minutes. Remove from the heat and cool slightly.

Put the squash pieces into a blender and add two-thirds of the mixture from the pan. Blitz until a purée forms, adding more of the liquid as necessary to make a thick spreadable purée. Set aside. The remaining liquid can be refrigerated and used as a seasoned stock.

Next, make the crispy cavolo nero topping. Use a small sharp knife to remove the thickest part of the stems. Use your hands to tear the leaves into rough pieces. Lay onto a well oiled baking sheet, and then sprinkle with a little salt and pepper. Mix well using your hands and then place in the preheated oven. Bake for 25–35 minutes until crispy and almost browning slightly.

In a small frying pan/skillet, add 1–2 tablespoons of olive oil and place on a high heat. When hot, add the sausage slices. Fry over a high heat to get the

edges to start to blacken slightly. Set aside on paper towels once browned.

When you are ready to make the flatbreads, preheat the oven to 220°C (425°F) Gas 7. Put a pizza stone into the hot oven for 10 minutes. Roll out one ball of dough to a rough oval about 20 x 15 cm/8 x 6 inches. Prick the surface in the middle of the dough with a fork to prevent bubbles. Dust the pizza stone or an upside-down baking sheet (or pizza paddle if you have one) with some polenta/cornmeal, then slide the dough onto the sheet.

To assemble, smear a few tablespoons of the squash purée over the bread, then scatter over some caramelized onion and blackened sausage and add some dollops of almond 'ricotta'. Bake in the preheated oven for 10–15 minutes until the crust is risen and browned.

Slide the flatbread onto a chopping board and sprinkle a handful of crispy cavolo nero and some toasted seeds over the top. Drizzle with chilli/chile oil and a final sprinkle of vegan Parmesan if you like.

THE BERLINER
MOCK 'DONER' KEBAB WITH SUMAC SLAW
& POMEGRANATE YOGURT SAUCE

I've eaten plenty of veggie and vegan kebabs/kabobs over the years, but there is a flavour profile and texture to kebab/kabob meat that I hadn't eaten in well over three decades until we visited Berlin and found ourselves enjoying fantastic mock meat as well as beer. We found vegan kebabs, burgers, doughnuts and a vegan weekend brunch spot with a queue winding down the street. Berlin really is a city is full of vegan surprises.

4 tablespoons flavourless coconut oil, or use solid vegetable fat, such as Trex
1 small carrot, peeled and finely chopped
120 g/4½ oz. dried TVP mince, soaked in 120 ml/ ½ cup boiling water with 1 teaspoon yeast extract/Marmite
3 teaspoons garlic powder
2 teaspoons onion powder
1½ teaspoons ground cumin
2 teaspoons ground coriander
2 teaspoons smoked paprika
2 teaspoons dried oregano or mixed herbs
1 teaspoon ground rainbow pepper
1 small onion, coarsely grated
75 g/2¾ oz. fresh breadcrumbs, white or brown
200 g/7 oz. vital wheat gluten
1 teaspoon salt
1 teaspoon freshly ground black pepper

FOR THE SLAW
2 tomatoes, roughly diced
1 red onion, roughly diced
¼ red cabbage, thinly sliced
¼ white cabbage, thinly sliced
handful of fresh mint leaves, roughly chopped
1–2 tablespoons pickled chillies/chiles
sea salt, to season

FOR THE SUMAC DRESSING
1 teaspoon ground sumac
juice of 1 orange
2 garlic cloves, chopped
1–2 tablespoons agave or maple syrup
2 tablespoons good quality olive oil
1 tablespoon balsamic vinegar

TO SERVE
150 g/⅔ cup vegan plain yogurt
75 g/2¾ oz. fresh pomegranate seeds
4 large vegan pitta breads
hot pepper sauce, such as Encona (optional)

small loaf pan, lightly oiled

SERVES 4

Put a medium frying pan/skillet over a medium-high heat and add the coconut oil or vegetable fat and carrot. Cook gently for 4–5 minutes. Drain the TVP mince, retaining the yeast broth. Add the mince to the pan along with the spices and seasoning and mix well. Cook for a minute or two, adding a splash of the broth to stop it sticking. Remove from the heat and then tip into a large, deep bowl. Add the onion, breadcrumbs and vital wheat gluten. Mix well, then add the yeast broth slowly to make a very firm dough. Mix well, then rest for 20–30 minutes in the fridge.

Preheat the oven to 160°C (325°F) Gas 3. Put the dough into the oiled loaf pan and tightly wrap with a layer of baking parchment, then a sheet of foil. Wrap tightly so it is a snug fit. Put the pan the preheated oven and bake for 2–3 hours.

Mix together all the slaw ingredients in a large bowl. Mix together the dressing ingredients and season to taste. Pour over the slaw and mix well. Set aside for at least 20–30 minutes.

Remove the loaf from the oven and leave to rest for 15 minutes. Unwrap and turn out.

Mix together the yogurt and pomegranate seeds in a small bowl, reserving a few of the seeds for garnishing. Cover and set aside.

Place the pittas into a medium oven or toaster and lightly brown for a few minutes. Slice open and fill with slaw as desired. Add generous layers of sliced 'doner meat', and slather with drizzles of pomegranate yogurt sauce. Scatter with a few mint leaves, pomegranate seeds and a drizzle of hot pepper sauce if you like. Serve immediately with napkins.

SEEKH KEBAB
IN MISSY ROTI

This Pakistani takeaway classic is traditionally made with minced lamb blended into an aromatic pulp and shaped onto long metal skewers. This vegan version is packed with all the flavours and can be chargrilled in exactly the same way for a delicious smoky flavour.

FOR THE KEBABS/KABOBS
100 g/3½ oz. TVP or soya mince, fresh, frozen or dried
1 teaspoon yeast extract/Marmite
120 g/4½ oz. chana dal (split yellow peas), soaked overnight
2 tablespoons fresh breadcrumbs
1 large onion, cut into 5 mm/¼ inch dice
1 tablespoon chickpea/gram flour
3 tablespoons freshly chopped coriander/cilantro
2 tablespoons ginger paste, or a large thumb-sized piece of fresh ginger, peeled and finely chopped
1 tablespoon garlic paste, or 6 garlic cloves, finely chopped
1–2 green chillies/chiles finely chopped
1½ teaspoons ground cumin, lightly toasted
3 teaspoons ground coriander, lightly toasted
½ teaspoon chilli powder
1–2 teaspoons salt, to taste

FOR THE RAITA
handful of coriander/cilantro, roughly chopped
handful of fresh mint, roughly chopped
6 tablespoons vegan plain yogurt
salt, to taste

FOR THE ROTI
240 g/9 oz. wholewheat chapati/atta flour
100 g/3½ oz. chickpea/gram flour
1½ teaspoons ajwain/carom seeds
1 onion, grated or finely chopped
2 green chillies/chiles, finely chopped
thumb-sized piece of fresh ginger, peeled and finely chopped
large pinch of asafoetida/hing
1–2 teaspoons salt, to taste
1 tablespoon vegetable oil, plus extra for frying

olive or vegetable oil, for grilling

4 kebab/kabob skewers

SERVES 4

Soak the dried TVP or soya mince in boiling water with the yeast extract/Marmite for 15 minutes. Drain the mince and squeeze out excess liquid. Drain the dal and blitz in a food processor to fine crumbs. Add to the bowl with the remaining kebab/kabob ingredients, mix well and set aside for 30–40 minutes.

Divide the mixture into four equal portions. Roll one portion into a ball and push onto a skewer. Then, using wet hands, squash the mixture to cover most of the skewer. Squeeze gently but firmly to get an even sausage shape along the skewer, then lay on greaseproof paper. Repeat with the other portions cover and leave to set in the fridge for 30 minutes.

To make the raita, blend the coriander/cilantro and mint to make a paste and then mix into the yogurt. Add salt to taste, then set aside.

To make the roti, combine the flours and ajwain/carom seeds in a large bowl and mix well. Add the remaining ingredients with 160 ml/generous ½ cup water. Knead into a pliable dough, adding more water as needed. Leave to rest for 15–20 minutes. Divide the dough into four balls and roll each ball out to a large disc approx. 5 mm/¼ inch thick. Heat the oil in a large frying pan/skillet over a medium-high heat and put one disc into the pan. Fry for 4–5 minutes until starting to brown at the edges and bubble slightly, then turn over and cook the second side for another 3–4 minutes, brushing regularly with oil. Lay on paper towels and repeat with the remaining roti.

To cook the kebabs/kabobs, brush the preheated BBQ/grill with oil. Lay a baking sheet underneath to catch any excess oil. Brush the kebabs/kabobs with oil and grill for 10–15 minutes, turning, until browned on all sides. Serve on top of a roti with salad and a drizzle of raita.

STICKY SEITAN CHKN HOT WINGS

I started developing 'wing' recipes a few years ago after I was approached by a couple of restaurateurs who were planning to open an organic vegan fast food joint in London. This is a simplified version of a tasty recipe that you can easily make at home. Making the wings can be a little fiddly but you can make them larger or thicker if you prefer.

FOR THE CHKN WINGS

200 g/7 oz. vital wheat gluten flour
2 tablespoons nutritional yeast
1 tablespoon onion powder
1 teaspoon Herbamere seasoning
½ teaspoon sea salt
½ teaspoon dried thyme
½ teaspoon dried marjoram
35 ml/2½ tablespoons tahini
150 ml/⅔ cup vegetable stock

FOR THE WET BATTER MIX

6 tablespoons flax egg
4 tablespoons chickpea/gram flour
2 tablespoons potato flour/starch
6 tablespoons hot pepper sauce, such as Encona
3 teaspoons Korean red pepper flakes

FOR THE DRY BATTER MIX

120 g/1 cup plain/all purpose flour
20 g/1¾ tablespoons potato flour/starch
2 tablespoons paprika
1 teaspoon freshly ground black pepper
1 teaspoon onion powder
½ teaspoon salt

FOR THE SAUCE

100 g/3½ oz. coconut butter, gently melted
150 ml/⅔ cup hot pepper sauce, such as Encona
2 tablespoons apple cider vinegar
1 teaspoon celery salt
2 teaspoons soy sauce
1 teaspoon paprika
1 teaspoon ground white pepper
1 teaspoon garlic powder

1.5 litres/6 cups vegetable stock
3–4 tablespoons sunflower or rapeseed oil, for frying
vegan ranch dip, to serve

MAKES APPROX. 24 WINGS

To make the wings, mix together the dry ingredients in a medium bowl. In a jug/pitcher, mix together the tahini and stock. Make a well in the centre of the bowl, and pour in the stock mixture. Combine the ingredients to make a stiff dough, adding two-thirds of the stock liquid. Add the remaining liquid if needed, the dough should be firm. Knead for a minute or two, then rest for 5–10 minutes.

Put the dough onto a well-floured surface and roll out to 2 cm/¾ inch thickness. To achieve a wing-like shape, use a heart-shaped cookie cutter, then make a small cut into the heart shape at the top. Press the dough down on the surface to flatten and shape.

Preheat the oven to 180°C (350°F) Gas 4. Add the vegetable stock to a deep baking pan and heat in the oven for 10 minutes. Remove the baking pan from the oven and place the chkn pieces into the water bath. Cover with foil and bake in the oven for 40 minutes. Remove the foil, then bake uncovered for a further 10–20 minutes. Remove the cooked chkn pieces and drain on paper towels.

Mix together the wet batter mix with 1–2 tablespoons of water. Add more water if needed but it should be fairly thick and cover a spoon well. In a small bowl combine the dry batter mix. Heat the oil in a deep pan or wok over a medium-high heat, 185°C (350°F) if using an electric fryer. Gently coat the chkn pieces in the wet batter mixture, then dip into the dry batter mixture. Shake gently to remove excess batter, then lay in the hot oil, frying for 3 minutes on each side until golden and crispy. Lay on paper towels to drain, then put on a baking sheet in a low oven while frying the remaining pieces in batches of four or five. Prepare the sauce by whisking together all the ingredients. Once all the chkn pieces are fried, place in a big bowl and pour over the wing sauce. Serve.

KFC-STYLE CHKN BURGER

They say the secret is the batter spicing, so it seems fair game to recreate this famous crispy coating into a classic burger sandwich. I've shortened the eleven herbs and spices, and added some more texture with cornflakes instead of chicken skin. This burger can be topped with barbecue, honey mustard or chilli/chili sauce, according to taste. Serve with fries for a faux fast food feast.

4 chkn escalopes (see page 13) or substitute 2-cm/¾-inch thick slices of 'chicken ham' (see page 14)
8 tablespoons aquafaba (see page 12) or use vegan 'egg' substitute, such as flax or Orgran
vegetable oil, for deep frying

FOR THE BUTTERMILK
250 ml/1 cup plus 1 tablespoon vegan milk, preferably almond
2 tablespoons vegan margarine, melted
1 tablespoon apple cider vinegar

FOR THE DRY FLOUR MIXTURE
1½ teaspoons salt
1 teaspoon dried mixed herbs
1 teaspoon celery salt
1 teaspoon freshly ground black pepper
1 teaspoon mustard powder

4 teaspoons paprika
2 teaspoons garlic salt
1 teaspoon ginger powder
3 teaspoons ground white pepper
100 g/¾ cup plain/all-purpose flour
60 g/2¼ oz. cornflour/cornstarch
1 teaspoon baking powder
75 g/2¾ oz. cornflakes, lightly crushed

TO SERVE
4 sesame burger rolls
6 tablespoons vegan mayonnaise
4 Batavia lettuce leaves, roughly torn
1 beef tomato, thinly sliced
2 tablespoons yellow mustard
chilli/chili or barbecue sauce

SERVES 4

First, make the buttermilk. Mix together the vegan milk with the melted margarine and apple cider vinegar. Put the chkn escalopes into the buttermilk mixture and set aside.

In a large bowl, add all the dry flour mixture ingredients, apart from the cornflakes, and mix well. Using one hand for the dry mixture and one for the buttermilk, lift the chkn escalopes from the milk into the flour mixture and toss well, ensuring they are very well coated. Once each escalope has been dipped once in the flour, add the cornflakes to the flour mixture and mix well. Dip the floured escalopes one at a time into the aquafaba or other vegan 'egg' substitute first, then into the cornflake and flour mixture so each has a nice crispy-textured coating. Repeat with all the escalopes. You can double dip if you like, to make a thicker crispy coating.

Heat the oil for frying to 180°C (350°F), and check the temperature with a cook's thermometer or by dropping a little cube of bread in the oil to check it is sizzling hot, but not burning. Fry each chkn escalope for 7–8 minutes until golden brown. Transfer to paper towels to drain off any excess oil.

To serve, slice the rolls in half and generously slather the bottom layers with mayonnaise. Put the lettuce on top of the mayonnaise, followed by the tomato and the crispy chkn on top. Top with mustard, chilli/chili or barbecue sauce, according to taste. Place the lids on top. Serve with fries.

JACKFRUIT CARNITAS

Carnitas are made with slow-cooked pork (or sometimes turkey or beef) and warm spices such as cinnamon and cloves. The meat is slow cooked until it has the traditional pulled consistency, and the meat is turned to ensure lots of crispy bits too. It is often served in soft flour tacos or on top of nachos with lime, coriander/cilantro and onion. I tried a version with wild mushroom in San Diego, but I think the dish lends itself really well to green jackfruit, with crispy sweet onions and hot fruity chilli/chili sauce to liven up the party.

1 large onion, thinly sliced
1 x 340-g/12-oz. can green jackfruit
1 tablespoon grated orange zest
6 garlic cloves, finely chopped
1 large onion, cut into 5-mm/¼-inch dice
1–2 teaspoons dried chilli/hot red pepper flakes
1 stick cinnamon or cassia bark
2 bay leaves
2 teaspoons dried oregano
pinch of ground cloves
½–1 teaspoon salt
vegetable oil, for frying

TO SERVE
20 small flour tortillas, approx. 15 cm/6 inches
4 tablespoons ancho chilli and mango dressing (see page 69), or use a hot pepper sauce, such as Encona
½ red onion, finely diced
handful of fresh coriander/cilantro
1 lime, cut into wedges

SERVES 4–6

Pour about 2.5 cm/1 inch of vegetable oil into a small pan and put over a high heat. When sizzling hot (but not burning), add the sliced onion and fry for 20–30 minutes until dark golden and crispy. Remove with a slotted spoon and lay on paper towels to drain.

Drain and rinse the jackfruit and place in a medium-sized pan with all the remaining ingredients and 355 ml/1½ cups water. Bring to a simmer over a medium-high heat and cook for 40 minutes until most of the water has evaporated. Remove the cinnamon or cassia bark and bay leaves.

Add a little splash of olive oil to the pan to stop it sticking and continue cooking the jackfruit so it starts to fry gently on a medium heat. This can take 5–10 minutes. Using a fork, break up the jackfruit so it has more of a 'pulled', slightly shredded appearance. Keep frying and allow some of the edges to brown a little before moving the crispy bits to the side and introducing new soft bits to the bottom. Continue this process for about 20–30 minutes until you have a mixture of crispy and soft bits. Remove from the heat and stir in 2 large tablespoons of the fried crispy onions. Taste and add more salt as you like.

Warm the tortillas and top each with generous spoonfuls of the jackfruit mixture. Scatter a few crispy onions on top, then drizzle with the ancho chilli and mango dressing and scatter the top with red onion and coriander/cilantro. Finish with a squeeze of lime and serve.

EASIEST VEGAN BURGER RECIPE EVER
WITH BEET KETCHUP

This quick and easy vegan burger is one of the simplest dishes to put together. Using gluten or seitan gives this patty a superbly meaty texture, with lots of smoky BBQ flavours in the mix. Apart from the seasonings, this vegan burger recipe has only five ingredients. This was a cupboard- and fridge-raider recipe, and so makes the perfect midweek easy supper. For that extra BBQ flavour, add a few droplets of liquid smoke to the final burger mix.

FOR THE PATTIES
coconut or vegetable oil, for frying
1 small onion, chopped
1 garlic clove, peeled and chopped
2 teaspoons smoked paprika
1 teaspoon salt
1 teaspoon ground white pepper
1 x 280-g/10-oz. can gluten/seitan, such as Mong Lee Shang vegetarian chicken or duck
1 x 240-g/8¾-oz. can red kidney beans, drained and rinsed
1 tablespoon soy sauce
50 g/½ cup chickpea/gram flour

FOR THE BEET KETCHUP
(MAKES 500 G/18 OZ. BATCH)
500 g/18 oz. beetroot/beets, peeled and diced
240 ml/1 cup apple cider vinegar
90 g/½ cup dark brown sugar
½ onion, diced
1 teaspoon salt
½ teaspoon ground white pepper
1 teaspoon ground coriander

TO SERVE
4 soft rolls
vegan mayo
lettuce leaves
tomato slices
red onion slices
sliced gherkins/pickles

SERVES 4

To make the beet ketchup, put all the ingredients into a pan and bring to a simmer over a medium-high heat. Reduce the heat and cook on low until the beetroot/beets are tender. Blitz with a stick blender until smooth. Season to taste, adding more salt or sugar as needed. Store in a sterilized glass jar. Will keep in the fridge for up to 1 month.

For the patties, place a small frying pan/skillet over a medium heat with the coconut or vegetable oil, and add the onion. Sauté for 10 minutes until translucent and sticky. Add the garlic, paprika, salt and pepper. Mix well and cook gently for 5–6 minutes. Remove from the heat.

Drain and rinse the canned gluten (or seitan). Using clean hands, shred into pieces.

Place the drained kidney beans in a bowl and pulp into rough chunky pieces using your hands or a fork.

In a large bowl, mix together all the patty ingredients including the soy sauce and chickpea/gram flour. Using your hands, knead the mixture together ensuring everything is mixed really well. Shape the mixture into four patties, and lay on greaseproof paper. Leave to set in the fridge for at least 20–30 minutes, longer if possible.

To cook the patties, add another tablespoon of oil to a large frying pan/skillet and fry them gently on each side for 6–7 minutes. Alternatively, preheat the oven to 180°C (350°F) Gas 4. Brush the patties well with oil and place on a baking sheet. Cook in the preheated oven for 25–30 minutes.

Serve with the ketchup in soft rolls with mayo, lettuce and slices of tomato, red onion and pickles.

KOREAN BARBECUE 'RIBS'

We only spent a couple of days in Asheville, North Carolina, but it was the last place I expected to be eating vegan Korean ribs. It was a happy accident that we ended up stopping off in this haven of counter-culture, so we made the most of eating out at some great vegan cafes and restaurants whilst exploring some of the Smoky Mountains.

This recipe is very easy to make, despite the long ingredients list. If you can't use a charcoal barbecue to cook these ribs, then a cast iron ridged griddle/grill pan works really well for adding a great smoky flavour.

FOR THE BBQ SAUCE
120 g/⅔ cup minus 2 teaspoons brown sugar
160 ml/⅔ cup soy sauce
1 tablespoon rice vinegar
2 generous tablespoons chilli/chili paste
2 heaped tablespoons gochujang
2 teaspoons sesame oil
1 teaspoon ground white pepper
thumb-sized piece of fresh ginger, peeled and finely chopped
6 garlic cloves, finely chopped
1–2 tablespoons cornflour/cornstarch

FOR THE 'RIBS' DRY MIX
150 g/5½ oz. vital wheat gluten flour
2 tablespoons chipotle powder
1 tablespoon onion powder
1 tablespoon garlic powder
1 tablespoon Korean red pepper chilli flakes

FOR THE WET MIX
2 tablespoons tahini
2 tablespoons tomato purée/paste
2 tablespoons umeboshi plum vinegar (or use apple cider vinegar)
2 tablespoons soy sauce
1 teaspoon smoked essence

TO SERVE
sesame seeds
3 spring onions/scallions, thinly sliced at angle (optional)
3–4 tablespoons kimchi
pinch of micro leaves or edible petals (optional)

2 lb. loaf pan, greased

MAKES APPROX. 8 RIBS

Put all the BBQ sauce ingredients except the cornflour/cornstarch, into a heavy-based pan with 60 ml/¼ cup water and put over a medium heat. Bring to a simmer and cook for about 30–40 minutes. Mix the cornflour/cornstarch with a little cold water to make a paste, then mix into the sauce to thicken. Simmer for a minute or two, stirring, then remove from the heat and set aside.

Preheat the oven to 175°C (325°F) Gas 3.

Mix together the dry mix ingredients in a large bowl. Mix the wet ingredients together in a jug/pitcher with 240 ml/1 cup water, and then pour into the dry ingredients. Mix well to form a sticky dough.

Grease a loaf pan and then tip the dough into the pan. Press the dough into the pan and flatten to make as smooth as possible. Bake in the preheated oven for about 40 minutes.

Remove from the oven and turn out onto a board. Slather generously all over with the BBQ sauce, then lay the slab of seitan on a preheat ridged griddle/grill pan or barbecue. Grill for a few minutes on each side, then remove and, using a sharp knife, slice the slab into 2.5-cm/1-inch thick ribs. Slather on some more sauce and return to the griddle/grill pan or barbecue. Grill for a few more minutes on each side until nicely crisped and browned. Sprinkle with sesame seeds, slices of spring onion/scallions and micro leaves or edible petals. Serve with kimchi and napkins.

COMFORT
FOOD CLASSICS

Anyone who has read *My Vegan Travels* will know how much I love my comfort food. I really enjoy re-inventing traditional dishes from brunches and family dinners that we tend to think of as conventionally meaty. Like many Brits, I'm a huge fan of the family brunch and Sunday roast dinners. I think we all adore the combination of getting together with loved ones over an abundance of good food. There are five vegetarians across my extended family, so I often prepare something special for us to enjoy in a family dinner with all the classic trimmings of roasties and seasonal veggies.

EX-BENEDICT

North-west Pacific-inspired brunching, and another vegan-take on a massive crowd-pleaser. The vegan hollandaise sauce can be used in other dishes. Delicious on asparagus, or add a little vinegar and tarragon for a vegan béarnaise.

FOR THE 'HOLLANDAISE'
360 ml/1½ cups unsweetened vegan milk (preferably almond)
1 tablespoon vegan 'egg' substitute, such as flax egg or Orgran
3 tablespoons vegan margarine
1 tablespoon plain/all-purpose flour
3 tablespoons freshly squeezed lemon juice
1 teaspoon sea salt
2 tablespoons vegan mayonnaise
¼ teaspoon chilli/chili powder

FOR THE 'OMELETTE'
175 g/1½ cups chickpea/gram flour
½ teaspoon baking powder
¼ teaspoon ground turmeric
large pinch of black salt
½ teaspoon ground white pepper
200 ml/generous ¾ cup water
vegetable oil, for frying

TO SERVE
2 English muffins, sliced and lightly toasted
handful of baby spinach leaves
4 mock smoky bacon rashers (see page 12), or use thickly sliced beef tomato
1 ripe avocado, peeled, pitted and thickly sliced (optional)
handful of freshly chopped chives (optional)

SERVES 4

Prepare the 'hollandaise' by whisking together the milk and vegan 'egg' substitute. In a small pan, add the margarine and flour and place on a low heat. Stir well to make a roux, then start slowing adding the milk mixture. Continue whisking while adding all the liquid, and bring to a simmer, cooking gently for a minute or two.

Turn down the heat to the lowest setting, then add the lemon juice, salt, mayo and chilli/chili powder. Whisk well. The sauce should be slightly thick and pourable. Add more mayo to thicken or more milk to thin slightly if needed.

Whisk together all the 'omelette' ingredients, except the oil, in a small bowl. Check the seasoning and add more salt as needed. Leave to stand for 5–10 minutes until it starts to bubble slightly. Place a small frying pan/skillet on a medium-high heat. Add a little vegetable oil and pour a small amount of batter into the centre of the pan. You can place a metal ring in the pan to shape the omelette to the size of the muffin, or simply pour the batter slowly into the centre until the desired size is reached. Fry for 3–4 minutes on each side, until cooked through and firm. Set aside on a baking sheet in a low oven while finishing the other omelettes.

For each serving, place one half of a muffin on a plate, and top with several spinach leaves and a rasher of vegan 'bacon' or a thick slice of beef tomato. Then place the 'omelette' round on top, then pour over a generous covering of 'hollandaise' sauce. Place a couple of slices of avocado on top and scatter with a few fresh chives if you like.

BOXTY IRISH PANCAKES
WITH SMOKY TEMPEH BACON, PUDDING & BEANS

We tend to associate the cooked breakfast as a Full English, but this breakfasting habit is actually as much loved across Ireland, Scotland and Wales too. Each have their own special take and additions. Growing up in an Irish family meant there was a lot of black and white puddings for me as a child, and the beloved boxty pancake!

These pancakes make a great alternative to toast, served with heaps of beans on top, or as part of a big cooked breakfast. Vegan black pudding has now become more readily available too and makes a delicious accompaniment.

FOR THE BOXTY PANCAKES
- 1–2 tablespoons vegan margarine, gently melted
- 210 ml/scant 1 cup unsweetened vegan milk
- 200 g/scant 1 cup cooked mashed potato
- 200 g/1½ cups raw grated potato
- 50 g/⅓ cup plain/all-purpose flour
- 1 teaspoon sea salt
- 1 teaspoon baking powder
- 2 spring onions/scallions, thinly sliced

FOR THE 'BACON'
- 2–4 tablespoons vegetable oil, for frying
- 350 g/12 oz. smoky tempeh
- 2 tablespoons soy sauce

TO SERVE
- 1 x 200-g/7-oz. packet of vegan black pudding (optional)
- 1 x 415-g/14½-oz. can baked beans, heated

SERVES 4

For the boxty pancakes, whisk the melted margarine into the milk and set aside.

In a large mixing bowl, add the potatoes, flour, salt and baking powder. Mix to combine well. Next, slowly add the milk mixture. Mix well but be careful not to overmix or the potato will become gluey. Carefully fold in the spring onions/scallions. The batter should be quite thick like lumpy porridge. Set aside.

For the 'bacon', slice the tempeh into 6 mm/¼ inch thick slices, and lay in a shallow dish. Pour over the soy sauce and leave to marinate for 5–10 minutes.

Add 2 tablespoons of the oil to a large frying pan/skillet and place over a medium heat. Add 2–3 generous tablespoons of batter for each pancake, spacing out in the pan to ensure enough room to cook and turn over. Fry each pancake for about 4–5 minutes on each side. The raw potato still needs to cook through, so be careful not to brown too quickly. Lay on a baking sheet and place in a low oven to keep warm while cooking the remaining pancakes.

Add a little more oil to the frying pan/skillet, and turn up the heat to medium-high. Add the tempeh slices and fry for 3–4 minutes on each side until starting to crisp and brown at the edges. If using black pudding, this can be cooked in the same pan. Slice thickly and fry according to instructions. Lay the tempeh and black pudding on paper towels to drain.

To serve, place a couple of pancakes onto each plate and top with several big spoonfuls of baked beans. Lay the bacon rashers on top. For this dish, I like to chop or crumble the black pudding (if using) into bite-sized pieces and scatter over the top.

Serve immediately.

MASALA CHICKPEA SCRAMBLE

Chickpea scrambles seemed to be the go-to vegan brunch along North America's West Coast. I tried my first tofu scramble in Portland, and came across the chickpea scramble several brunches later. These are especially delicious when the chickpeas are well seasoned, and I love masala-style spice for brekko more than anything. Adding the aubergine/eggplant gives a creamier fluffy texture. I like to serve with crispy sautéed potatoes for a weekend treat.

1 small aubergine/
   eggplant, thickly sliced
   into 2–3-cm/
   ¾–1¼-inch pieces
½ teaspoon smoked
   paprika
1½ teaspoons salt
1 x 400-g/14-oz. can
   chickpeas, drained and
   rinsed
½ teaspoon ground
   turmeric
½ teaspoon ground
   cumin
2 tablespoons freshly
   squeezed lemon juice
1 tablespoon tahini
1 garlic clove, finely
   chopped
1 tablespoon vegetable
   oil
2.5-cm/1-inch piece of
   fresh ginger, peeled
   and finely chopped, or
   substitute ½ teaspoon
   ground ginger

2 green chillies/chiles,
   chopped, plus extra
   to garnish if desired
2 spring onions/scallions,
   thinly sliced
8 cherry tomatoes,
   halved
2 handfuls of baby
   spinach leaves
thick granary toast or
   sautéed potatoes,
   to serve
handful of fresh
   coriander/cilantro
   leaves

lightly oiled baking sheet

SERVES 2–3

Preheat the oven to 200°C (400°F) Gas 6.

Place the aubergine/eggplant slices on a lightly oiled baking sheet and sprinkle with the paprika and 1 teaspoon of the salt. Bake in the preheated oven for 15–20 minutes until completely softened. Remove and set aside to cool.

Using a fork, mash the chickpeas to a chunky pulp. Add the salt, remaining turmeric and cumin, then mix well and set aside.

Peel off the skin from the aubergine/eggplant pieces. It doesn't matter if a little skin remains. Blitz the aubergine/eggplant in a food processor, along with the lemon juice, tahini and garlic to make a thick purée (essentially a baba ganoush dip).

Place a frying pan/skillet on a medium heat and heat the vegetable oil. Add the ginger, chillies/chiles and whites of the spring onions/scallions. Fry gently for 3–4 minutes until the onions start to soften, then add the chickpea mixture. Cook for a few minutes.

Add the aubergine/eggplant purée, then the tomatoes, mixing well, and as soon as everything is heated through, serve on top of baby spinach and thick granary toast or sautéed potatoes. Scatter with fresh coriander/cilantro leaves and extra chillies/chiles if you like.

MUSHROOM 'STEAK' & FRITES

This vegan take on an ultimately classic French dish will probably upset some of my omni chef friends. Portobello mushrooms are incredibly meaty in flavour and texture, and often served whole by restaurants as a quick and cheap substitute for a burger. Of course, these mushroom 'steaks' are not the texture of actual beef, but they are juicy and flavoursome, and can be shaped into vegan burger patties or served like a steak with your favourite sauce, such as peppercorn. They can also be made in advance, cooked and then frozen for a month or two.

6 Portobello mushrooms, cleaned
4 tablespoons flavourless coconut oil, gently melted
2 red onions, finely diced
2–3 garlic cloves, peeled and chopped
½ small glass of red wine, (optional)
240 g/9 oz. cooked black beans, mashed
45 g/1½ oz. rolled/ old-fashioned oats
3 tablespoons aquafaba (see page 12) or other vegan 'egg' substitute
45 g/generous ½ cup fresh breadcrumbs
1 heaped tablespoon steak seasoning
1 tablespoon Henderson's Relish
1 tablespoon dark soy sauce
2 tablespoons tapioca starch
1 tablespoon chickpea/ gram flour

FOR THE FRITES
2 large baking potatoes
1 teaspoon salt
vegetable oil, for deep frying

TO SERVE
peppercorn sauce (optional)
ketchup and vegan mayonnaise (optional)
rocket/arugula leaves

SERVES 3–4

Prepare the frites by peeling the potatoes and cutting them into 4-mm/⅛-inch wide matchsticks. I like to use large baking potatoes, so the frites are nice and long. Place them in a bowl of cold water to stop them browning.

Heat the vegetable oil in a large pan or wok to approx. 165˚C/325˚F.

Drain the potato matchsticks and pat dry. Fry them, in batches if needed, taking care not to crowd the pan. Cook for 3–4 minutes. They should not brown at all, but still be almost cooked. Remove and drain on paper towels.

Trim the gills from the mushrooms, then dice the stems and cups into ½–1 cm/¼–⅜ inch pieces. Place a small frying pan/skillet over a medium heat and add 2 tablespoons of the coconut oil. Add the onions and soften slightly for a few minutes. Then add the garlic and wine, if using, and cook for another 2–3 minutes over a high heat to reduce all the liquid. Remove from the heat.

Tip the onion mixture into a large bowl and add all the remaining ingredients including the remaining coconut oil. Wet your hands, and then mix well. Shape the mixture into burger-like patties.

Place a large frying pan/skillet onto a medium heat and add 2 tablespoons of oil. Gently fry the patties for 3–5 minutes on each side until they are just browning.

Meanwhile, heat up the oil for the frites to 190˚C (375˚F) and cook the fries for a second time for 2–3 minutes until golden and crispy. Drain on paper towels, then season well with salt. Serve immediately.

SMOKY STUFFED ROAST
WITH PINE NUT, LEMON & HERB

Home-smoking is very easy and adds a deep layer of flavour to lots of dishes, including homemade vegan meats or cheeses. I use an large lidded pan (only used for smoking) and a steamer basket – the kind that makes a raised layer and adjusts to the size of the pan. Smoking chips are available from cook shops or online. You can cheat by adding smoked essence to the mixture, but this doesn't infuse in the same flavourful way as actual smoking.

FOR THE ROASTING PAN
1 litre/1 quart vegetable stock
2 onions, quartered, skin on
1 glass of white wine (optional)
2 tablespoons soy sauce
handful of fresh herbs, such as thyme and rosemary
1 garlic bulb, halved
1–2 lemons, halved
1 tablespoon olive or vegetable oil
2 tablespoons balsamic vinegar

FOR THE STUFFING
2 tablespoons olive oil
2 small onions, diced
4 garlic cloves, crushed
2 slices white or brown bread
12 fresh sage leaves, finely chopped
½ teaspoon chopped zest and freshly squeezed juice of ½ lemon
½-1 teaspoon salt
½ teaspoon freshly ground black pepper
50 g/⅓ cup pine nuts

FOR THE DRY RUB
1 teaspoon ground white pepper
1 teaspoon freshly ground black pepper
2 teaspoons dried herbs
1 teaspoon salt

FOR THE ROAST
400 g/14 oz. vital wheat gluten flour
45 g/⅓ cup chickpea/gram flour
2 teaspoons garlic powder
2 tablespoons nutritional yeast
1 tablespoon onion powder
2 teaspoons Herbamere seasoning
1 teaspoon dried mixed herbs
60 ml/¼ cup tahini
280–400 ml/10–14 fl. oz. vegetable stock
2 teaspoons smoked essence (optional)

large muslin/cheesecloth sheet, approx. 60 cm/ 24 inches square
twine or string
large handful of smoking chips and foil (or substitute 3 teaspoons smoked essence)
large lidded pan and metal steaming basket

SERVES 7–8

Preheat the oven to 180°C (350°F) Gas 4.

Add all the roasting pan ingredients into a large deep pan with 1 litre/1 quart water and set aside.

To make the stuffing, in a large frying pan/skillet, add the olive oil, onions and garlic and fry over a low heat for about 8–10 minutes until well softened. Turn up the heat to medium-high and continue to fry the mixture so that the onions start to brown slightly. Remove the pan from the heat and tip the contents into a large bowl. Leave to cool.

Blitz the slices of bread in a food processor to make fine breadcrumbs. Add these to the stuffing mixture, along with the sage, lemon zest and juice, salt and pepper. Roughly chop the pine nuts and add to the bowl. Mix well with your hands. Set aside.

To make the roast, mix together the dry ingredients in a medium bowl. In a jug/pitcher, mix together the tahini and stock (add the smoked essence at this point if using). Make a well in the centre of the bowl, and pour in ⅔ of the stock mixture. Combine the ingredients to make a stiff dough. Add the remaining liquid if needed; the dough should be nice and firm. Knead well for a minute or two, then leave to rest for 5–10 minutes.

Place the dough on the work surface and roll out to an oblong shape about 2–3 cm/¾–1¼ inches thick. It is very springy to work with so you will need to be patient and firm. Mix together the dry rub ingredients and scatter on the work surface. Place the flattened dough piece onto the dry rub. Press down slightly, then lift and place, rub-side down, onto a very well-oiled muslin/cheesecloth.

Scoop up the stuffing using your hands and make a fat sausage shape of stuffing down the centre of the dough. Carefully roll the gluten dough up around the stuffing, using the muslin/cheesecloth to help you. Try to seal the ends as much as possible. Twist the ends of the cloth to make a tight fat sausage shape. Tie with twine to secure. Add an additional loop around the centre of the roast if needed.

Place the roast into the prepared roasting pan. Cover with foil and bake in the preheated oven for 1 hour 50 minutes. Turn once halfway through cooking. Remove the foil cover and return to the oven for a further 30–40 minutes, turning the oven up to 200˚C (400˚F) Gas 6. Then remove from the pan and set aside to cool slightly on a plate for about 1 hour. Remove the muslin/cheesecloth.

Lay out a large square of foil and place a handful of smoking chips in the centre. Spread out slightly and then wrap the foil around to create a fairly flat parcel. Lay in the bottom of the smoking pan, and stab a few small holes in the top of the foil. Lay the steamer basket on top of the foil package and place the roasted joint on top of this. Put on the lid of the pan and place on a high heat on the hob/stovetop. It usually takes about 5–6 minutes to create enough heat to start the chips smoking. Once they start to smoke, turn down the heat to low, but do not remove the lid as the smoke needs to stay trapped inside the pan. After another 5–10 minutes, I place the pan outside in the garden (but you can keep it indoors off the heat). Leaving the lid on, leave it to smoke away for 20 minutes or so on its own. The longer you leave it to smoke (reheating the chips periodically in between), the stronger the smoky flavour will be.

Remove the roast from the pan. To reheat for serving, the roast can be placed back into a roasting pan, covered with foil and then warmed in the oven at 170˚C (325˚F) Gas 3 for 10–15 minutes or warmed in the microwave on High for 2–3 minutes. Serve in thick slices with mashed potato and miso gravy.

CELEBRATION WELLINGTON

The Wellington is an instantly recognisable sign of a celebratory feast. It's an impressive dish to bring to the table too. I developed this recipe for the Annual Dinner for Victoria's Promise, a charity that provides support to young women with cancer. They wanted an example of how vegan food can be as impressive as a meat roast, but wanted a recipe that was also fairly traditional and familiar for a range of dinner guests. The roast in the middle can also be served without all the pastry fanfare too, for a more straightforward Sunday dinner. I usually make at least two of the roasts, and freeze one for up to 2 months. The mushroom pâté is delicious as a dip or in a sandwich too. Definitely worth doubling the quantity, as it freezes well or keeps in the fridge for up to a week.

FOR THE ROAST

500 g/18 oz. vital wheat gluten flour

45 g/⅓ cup chickpea/gram flour

5 tablespoons flavourless coconut oil

2 banana shallots, finely chopped

1 medium leek, finely chopped

150 g/5½ oz. chestnut mushrooms, finely chopped

150 g/5 oz. field or Portobello mushrooms, finely chopped

6 garlic cloves, finely chopped

2 teaspoons garlic powder

3 g/⅛ oz. dried porcini or wild mushrooms, soaked in 100 ml/⅓ cup plus 1 tablespoon boiling water

1 tablespoon tomato purée/paste

2 teaspoons sea salt

½ tablespoon Marmite or other yeast extract

1½ tablespoons dark soy sauce

4 bay leaves

1 small glass of robust red wine, such as Syrah (approx. 100 ml/⅓ cup plus 1 tablespoon)

150 ml plus 50 ml/⅔ cup plus 3½ tablespoons roasted vegetable stock

1 teaspoon smoked essence

1 teaspoon fine sea salt

FOR THE DRY RUB

2 teaspoons freshly ground black pepper

2 teaspoons paprika

1 teaspoon ground white pepper

2 teaspoons dried mixed herbs

For the roast, put the gluten and chickpea/gram flour in a large mixing bowl. Mix together and set aside.

In a medium frying pan/skillet, add half the coconut oil, the shallots and leek, then place over a medium heat. Sauté for 7–9 minutes to soften the vegetables, then add the mushrooms and fresh and powdered garlic. Chop the soaked dried mushrooms and add them along with the soaking liquid to the pan. Cook for 6–7 minutes, then add the remaining coconut oil, tomato purée/paste, salt, Marmite/yeast extract, soy sauce, bay leaves, smoked essence and red wine. Bring to a simmer, stirring well, then reduce the liquid by half on a high heat for another 5–10 minutes, then set aside to cool.

Preheat the oven to 180°C (350°F) Gas 4. Add all the roasting pan ingredients into a large, deep roasting pan and set aside.

Add the mushroom mixture along with the 150 ml/⅔ cup vegetable stock to the gluten and chickpea/gram flour, mixing well to make a very stiff dough. Add a little more liquid if needed, depending on the flour density and mushrooms. The stiffer the dough, the firmer the texture of the vegan 'meat'. Knead well for a few minutes to ensure it is well mixed. You can also use a stand mixer and dough hook for this. Roll the dough into a large, thick roast shape and then leave to rest for about 10 minutes.

Mix together the dry rub ingredients and scatter on the work surface. Roll the dough in this dry rub,

FOR THE ROASTING PAN

450 ml/scant 2 cups
  good-quality vegetable
  stock
2 small onions, quartered,
  skins left on
1 small glass of robust
  red wine, such as Syrah
  (approx. 100 ml/⅓ cup
  plus 1 tablespoon)
2 tablespoons soy sauce
handful of fresh thyme
2–3 fresh rosemary
  sprigs
1 tablespoon olive or
  vegetable oil
1 tablespoon balsamic
  vinegar

FOR THE PATE

250 g/9 oz. field,
  Portobello or chestnut
  mushrooms, cleaned
handful of fresh parsley
80 g/⅔ cup pecans,
  lightly toasted
  (or use walnuts)
40 g/3 tablespoons
  vegan margarine
salt and ground white
  pepper, to taste

TO MAKE THE PANCAKES

125 g/1 cup minus
  1 tablespoon plain/
  all-purpose flour
1 flax egg (see page 12)
240 ml/1 cup
  unsweetened soy milk
flavourless coconut oil or
  vegetable oil, for frying
vegetable oil, for
  brushing

1 x 500-g/18-oz. packet
  of ready-made vegan
  puff pastry
4 tablespoons soy milk
1 teaspoon black poppy
  seeds
plain/all-purpose flour,
  for dusting

1 large muslin/
  cheesecloth sheet,
  approx. 60 cm/
  24 inches square
twine or string for tying

SERVES 7–8

then lay on the lightly oiled muslin/cheesecloth and roll so the roast is snugly wrapped in the cloth. Tie each end with twine. Tie further loops around the roast to ensure it is fairly tightly wrapped and secure. Lay the roast in the roasting pan, cover the pan with foil and place in the oven for 2 hours. Turn once halfway through cooking. Remove the foil and return to the oven for further 30–40 minutes, then remove and set aside to cool slightly for about an hour. Then remove muslin/cheesecloth.

Preheat the oven to 120°C (250°F) Gas ½. To make the pâté, lay the mushrooms on a dry baking sheet and place in the oven for 30–40 minutes, occasionally draining away the liquid from the baking sheet. Once roasted and fairly dry-looking, blitz together with the parsley, pecans and margarine using a food processor or stick blender. Season with salt and pepper to taste. Set aside in the fridge to chill.

Make the pancakes by whisking together the flour, flax egg and soy milk. In a small frying pan/skillet, add a knob of coconut oil or a little veg oil and place over a high heat. Pour a small amount of batter into the pan, using a spatula to spread the batter thinly across the base of the pan. Cook for a few minutes on each side. Set aside to cool on paper towels. Repeat.

Roll out the puff pastry to a rectangle of about 3–4 mm/⅛ inch thickness. Lay the pancakes over the top of the pastry, so they are slightly overlapping and cover most of the pastry apart from the edges. Thickly spread the mushroom pâté over the pancakes, then gently lay the roast in the centre. Wrap the pancake and pastry layers around the roast, using the soy milk to seal. Trim the pastry to make neatly folded ends. Glaze the outside of the pastry with soy milk. Sprinkle with poppy seeds, and score the pastry if you like. Set on a baking sheet and place in the oven at 180°C (350°F) Gas 4 for 20–30 minutes until pastry is puffed and crisp.

Strain the roasting pan juices into a small pan and bring to a simmer with a little flour to thicken if needed. Once the roast is cooked, carve and serve.

CORNED BEEFY HASH

This recipe uses the same roast recipe from the Wellington (see pages 121–122), but simply changes the dry rub mixture, and the roasting pan ingredients have been rebooted with the addition of some beloved Guinness. You could substitute ready-made vegan beef pieces and add a teaspoon of the dry rub ingredients to the pan (and a splash of the dark stuff!). Using traditional corned beef flavours in the spices imparts some familiar flavours into this vegan-take on an Irish classic. Serve with some fried cabbage.

400 g/14 oz. roast recipe
(see pages 121–122)
2 large potatoes, peeled and cubed
1 tablespoon olive oil, plus extra for drizzling
1 onion, thickly sliced
1 green (bell) pepper, cored, deseeded and thickly diced
2 tablespoons Henderson's Relish or vegan Worcestershire sauce
½ teaspoon freshly ground black pepper
½–1 teaspoon sea salt, to taste

FOR THE DRY RUB
2 teaspoons black mustard seeds
1 teaspoon freshly ground black pepper
1 teaspoon ground allspice
½ teaspoon ground ginger
pinch of ground cinnamon

FOR THE ROASTING PAN
450 ml/scant 2 cups good-quality vegetable stock
1 tablespoon sea salt
1 onion, quartered, skin left on
1 large can of Guinness (which is vegan in UK and Eire) or other dark stout
1 teaspoon dried juniper berries
1 tablespoon olive or vegetable oil
½ teaspoon whole cloves

medium muslin/cheesecloth sheet, approx. 40.5 cm/16 inches square, lightly oiled
twine, for tying

SERVES 4

Preheat the oven to 180°C (350°F) Gas 4. Add all the roasting pan ingredients into a large, deep roasting pan and set aside.

First, make the roast recipe (see pages 121–122).

Mix together the dry rub ingredients and scatter on the work surface. Roll the dough in the dry rub, then lay on the lightly oiled muslin/cheesecloth and roll so the roast is snugly wrapped in the cloth. Tie each end with twine. Tie further loops around the roast to ensure it is fairly tightly wrapped and secure. Lay the roast in the prepared roasting pan, cover the pan with foil and place in the preheated oven for 2 hours. Turn once halfway through cooking. Remove the foil cover and return to the oven for a further 30–40 minutes, then remove and set aside to cool slightly for about 1 hour. Then remove the muslin/cheesecloth.

Slice the roast into four big pieces and then, using a knife or your hands, slice or tear the roast pieces into large chunks. You will only need 400 g/14 oz. of the roasted chunks for this dish to serve 4. The remaining roast can be frozen for several months.

Place a medium pan half-filled with water over a high heat. Bring to the boil and add the potatoes. Boil for about 8–10 minutes until just softening, then drain and set aside.

In a large frying pan/skillet, add the olive oil and then the onion and (bell) pepper. Fry for 2–3 minutes, then add the potatoes and fry for another 8–10 minutes until lightly browned. Season. Add the roasted chunks and mix well, frying on a high heat. Finally, drizzle with a little olive oil, mix well and serve immediately with Henderson's Relish on the side.

GREEN JACKFRUIT & 3 BEAN CHILLI
WITH CORNBREAD DUMPLINGS

This deeply rich and satisfying recipe is pure comfort food, and the chilli/chili itself can be used in several other dishes, such as a burrito (see page 87) or as a fast food-style topping on burgers and hotdogs (see page 80). It will keep in the fridge for up to a week and freezes well for several months. Whilst this looks like a long list of ingredients, the actual recipe is a very simple 'chuck it all in the pot' kind of dish.

2–3 tablespoons vegetable oil

2 red onions, finely diced

2 small yellow onions, finely diced

1 celery stick/stalk, finely diced

1 large carrot, peeled and finely diced

4 garlic cloves, chopped

1 red (bell) pepper, cored, deseeded and finely diced

1 large red chilli/chile, finely diced

1 teaspoon chipotle chilli/chili powder

2 teaspoons ground cumin

1 teaspoon ground coriander

1 teaspoon hot smoked paprika

2 teaspoons paprika

1 teaspoon dried oregano

3 tablespoons tomato purée/paste

1 x 280-g/10-oz. can green jackfruit, drained and rinsed, then roughly chopped

1 litre/1 quart vegetable stock

1 tablespoon dark soy sauce

½ teaspoon Marmite or yeast extract

1 x 240-g/9-oz. can red kidney beans, drained and rinsed

1 x 400-g/14-oz. can chickpeas, drained and rinsed

1 x 400-g/14-oz. can borlotti or rosecoco beans, drained and rinsed

1 x 400-g/14-oz. can plum tomatoes, squashed

2 large chunks of vegan dark chocolate (at least 75% cocoa solids)

FOR THE DUMPLINGS

160 g/generous 1 cup polenta/cornmeal

200 g/1½ cups self-raising/self-rising flour

60 g/¼ cup vegan margarine or suet

1½ teaspoons baking powder

90 g/1 packed cup grated vegan cheese (such as violife)

large handful of freshly chopped coriander/cilantro

½ teaspoon sea salt

150 ml/⅔ cup unsweetened soy milk

TO SERVE

dollop of Oatly crème fraîche or vegan soured/sour cream

SERVES 6

Prepare the chilli by placing a large, heavy-based saucepan over a medium heat. Add the vegetable oil and then add the onions, celery and carrot. Sauté for 7–8 minutes, then add the garlic, red (bell) pepper and chilli/chile. Cook gently for about 10 minutes until all the vegetables are well softened.

Add the dried spices and herbs, stir well. Then add the tomato purée/paste and mix well. Cook for a few minutes before adding the jackfruit and the stock. Bring to the boil and simmer for about 10–15 minutes until the jackfruit has softened, then add all the remaining chilli ingredients, except the chocolate. Bring back to a simmer, and cook gently with a lid on for about 20–25 minutes. Add the chocolate pieces at the end of cooking and mix in well.

Meanwhile, prepare the cornbread dumplings. Mix the polenta/cornmeal, baking powder and flour together in a bowl. Rub the margarine into the flours (just add the suet loose if using). Then mix in the baking powder, vegan cheese, chopped coriander/cilantro and salt. Add the soy milk to the dry ingredients, mixing well to make a soft dough. Add a little more milk if the dumpling dough is too dry.

Dip your hands into cold water, then roll the dough into eight balls and place on top of the chilli (give the chilli a really good stir before you top it with the dumplings, using a fork to break up the jackfruit slightly if you want the pulled pork-like texture). Replace the lid and cook for another 20–25 minutes until the dumplings are risen and cooked.

Serve with a dollop of Oatly crème fraîche or vegan soured/sour cream and a green salad.

TOAD-IN-THE-HOLE
WITH GARDEN SAUSAGES & ROASTED ONION GRAVY

I served this vegan Yorkshire pudding recipe as part of a huge Christmas banquet. We made miniature toad-in-the-holes with little vegan chipolatas, as part of our 17 dish Vegan Extravaganzo Pop-Up, with my dessert pal BakeOrama (aka Charlotte O' Toole). I made so many versions of the batter before I perfected it. The recipe for the batter is a little more exacting and for once I recommend you don't deviate if you want to achieve a fluffy pudding-like texture. The result is more popover than pudding (and may bury your sausages), but it's light and crispy-edged with a Yorkie pud-like flavour and texture.

FOR THE SAUSAGES
175 g/6 oz. frozen vegan mince or 90 g/3¼ oz. dried textured vegetable protein (TVP), 1 teaspoon Marmite/yeast extract and 2 tablespoons soy sauce
4 tablespoons olive oil
2 shallots, finely diced
4 garlic cloves, peeled and chopped
1 large carrot, diced
1 leek, thinly sliced
1 medium potato, peeled and diced into 4-mm/⅛-inch cubes
3 teaspoons garlic powder
1 teaspoon onion powder
9 fresh sage leaves, chopped, or 1 teaspoon dried sage
small handful of fresh thyme, chopped, or 1 teaspoon dried thyme
1 teaspoon liquid smoke
100–200 ml/⅓–1 cup vegetable stock
150 g/5½ oz. vital wheat gluten flour
2 tablespoons chickpea/gram flour
sea salt and freshly ground black pepper

FOR THE GRAVY
2 tablespoons olive oil
3 red onions, thinly sliced
2 tablespoons plain/all-purpose flour
1 small glass of red wine (optional)
1 tablespoon soy sauce
1 teaspoon garlic powder
1 litre/1 quart roasted vegetable stock
½ teaspoon ground white pepper

FOR THE PUDDING BATTER
1–2 tablespoons vegetable fat, such as Trex
150 g/1 cup plus 1 tablespoon self-raising/self-rising flour
320 ml/11 fl oz. unsweetened soy milk
2 teaspoons baking powder
¼ teaspoon bicarbonate of soda/baking soda
½ teaspoon black salt
60 ml/¼ cup aquafaba (see page 12), whipped into soft peaks

6–8 squares of greaseproof paper
6–8 squares of foil
25.5 cm/10 inch wide ovenproof dish

SERVES 4

For the sausages, if using frozen vegan mince, ensure it is fully defrosted. If using dried TVP, simmer for 5–10 minutes in a small pan with 710 ml/3 cups of boiling water along with the Marmite/yeast extract and soy sauce. Leave to stand for a few minutes, then strain.

In a medium frying pan/skillet, add the oil, shallots, garlic, carrot and leek and place over a medium heat. Fry gently for 7–8 minutes and then add the potato pieces. Cook for another 10 minutes until all the vegetables are softened but the potatoes are only just cooked. Add the garlic and onion powders, mince, fresh or dried herbs, liquid smoke, and salt and pepper. Stir well so all the flavours are well combined, then add 60 ml/¼ cup of the stock. Check the seasoning of the mixture and add more salt if needed. Remove from the heat, tip into a large bowl and cool the mixture for 10–15 minutes.

Add the wheat gluten, chickpea/gram flour and mince mixture to the bowl and combine to make a dough. Add the remaining stock, as much as needed to make a firm dough. I suggest adding 2–3 tablespoons at a time until the dough comes together. Combine well and then divide the dough into 6–8 pieces and roll roughly into sausage shapes. Using the greaseproof squares, roll each sausage inside a paper square, achieving a more even shape and desired size, approx. 12–14 cm/4¾ x 5½ inches long. Roll in the paper and then twist the ends to secure. Wrap in foil and roll again, wrapping and twisting the ends like a cracker. Repeat to make

6–8 wrapped sausages. Place the sausages in the fridge for 30–40 minutes, longer if possible.

To make the gravy, in a heavy-based pan, add 2 tablespoons olive oil along with the sliced red onions. Fry over a medium-high heat for 12–15 minutes until well softened and browned. Then add the plain flour and mix well. Cook for a minute or two, then add the wine, soy sauce, garlic powder, stock and pepper. Bring to a simmer, and cook over a low heat for 20–30 minutes. Taste and season with more soy sauce and pepper if you like. Set aside, reheating as needed just before serving.

Once the sausages have set, remove from the fridge, place in a steamer and cook for 1 hour. Once cooked, allow to cool before removing the foil and paper wrapping. This is the best stage for freezing the sausages if you have made a large batch. They will keep in the freezer for several months.

Preheat the oven to 220°C (425°F) Gas 7.

Put 1–2 tablespoons olive oil into a small, non-stick pan over a medium heat. Add the sausages and cook for 7–8 minutes until lightly browned on all sides. Set aside.

Put the vegetable fat into the ovenproof dish and put on the middle shelf in the oven.

To make the pudding batter, sift the flour into a large bowl and whisk together with the rest of the batter ingredients, except the aquafaba. Whisk well to make the mixture slightly frothy. Then gently fold in the aquafaba. Remove the hot baking dish from the oven and place on top of the hob/stovetop. Pour the frothy batter mixture into the hot dish, then top with 6–8 of the sausages. It should sizzle and bubble. Carefully and quickly place the dish back in the hot oven. Bake undisturbed for 25–35 minutes, until the batter is cooked through and crispy.

Serve with the hot onion gravy and steamed greens such as sprouting broccoli stems.

ITALIAN-STYLE BEAN CASSEROLE
WITH ROASTED GARLIC & ARTICHOKE SAUSAGES

This warming 'cassoulet'-style base can be eaten with or without the sausages. It's super simple to make but just requires the soaking and cooking times, so the flavours are well cooked and the beans are meltingly soft. I sometimes make this base using green or brown lentils too. You can add 'lardons' of mock bacon/ham (see pages 12 and 14) or roasted potato pieces if you like too. Serve with warm crusty bread.

FOR THE BEAN CASSEROLE
150 g/generous 1 cup dried black-eyed beans/black-eyed peas, soaked in cold water overnight

150 g/generous 1 cup haricot/navy beans, soaked in cold water overnight

4 garlic cloves, chopped

2 small carrots, diced into 1-cm/½-inch cubes

1 large celery stick/stalk, plus handful of leaves, roughly chopped

3 shallots, finely diced

small handful of fresh thyme leaves, or 1 tablespoon dried thyme

900 ml/scant 4 cups good-quality vegetable stock

2 tablespoons olive oil

small bunch of cavolo nero, roughly chopped

FOR THE SAUSAGES
175 g/6 oz. frozen vegan mince or 100 g/3½ oz. dried textured vegetable protein (TVP), 1 teaspoon Marmite/yeast extract and 2 tablespoons dark soy sauce

1 garlic bulb, roasted whole with skin left on

4 tablespoons olive oil

2 shallots, finely diced

1 x 280-g/10-oz. jar artichoke hearts in olive oil, drained and roughly chopped

1 teaspoon onion powder

leaves from 1 sprig of fresh rosemary

leaves from 3 sprigs of fresh thyme

1 teaspoon sea salt

20–30 ml/4–6 teaspoons vegetable stock

80 g/3 oz. vital wheat gluten flour

1 tablespoon chickpea/gram flour

freshly ground black pepper, to taste

handful of freshly chopped parsley, to serve

crusty bread, to serve

6–8 squares of greaseproof paper
6–8 squares of foil

SERVES 4

For the bean casserole, rinse and drain the beans, and put in a large, deep pan. Cover the beans generously with water and place over a high heat. Bring to the boil and use a large spoon to remove any scum from the top of the water. Simmer for approx. 30–40 minutes until the beans are just soft. Remove from the heat and drain in a colander. Set aside.

For the sausage, if using frozen vegan mince, ensure it is fully defrosted. If using dried TVP, simmer for 5–10 minutes in a small pan with 710 ml/3 cups of boiling water along with the Marmite/yeast extract and soy sauce.

Preheat the oven to 200°C (400°F) Gas 6. Put the whole garlic cloves (with skin on) onto a baking sheet and put in the preheated oven. Bake for 15–20 minutes until well roasted and sticky soft. Set aside to cool.

In a medium frying pan/skillet, add the oil and shallots and place over a medium heat. Fry gently for 7–8 minutes and then add the artichoke pieces. Cook for another 10 minutes until all the vegetables are softened.

Peel and chop the roasted the garlic and add to the pan along with the onion powder, mince, herbs, salt and some pepper. Stir well so all the flavours are well combined, then add the 20 ml/ 4 teaspoons of the stock. Check the seasoning of the mixture and add more salt if needed. Remove from the heat, tip into a large bowl and cool the mixture for 10–15 minutes.

Add the wheat gluten and chickpea/gram flour to the bowl and combine to make a dough. Add the

remaining stock as needed to make a firm dough. Knead for a minute or two and then divide the dough into 8 pieces and roughly roll into sausage shapes. Using the greaseproof squares, roll each sausage inside a paper square, achieving a more even shape and desired size, approx. 12–14 cm/4¾–5½ inches long. Roll in the paper and then twist the ends to secure. Wrap in foil and roll again, wrapping and twisting the ends like a cracker. Repeat with the remaining sausages. Place the sausages in the fridge for 30–40 minutes, longer if possible.

Once the sausages have set, remove from the fridge and place in a steamer and cook for an hour. Once cooked, allow to cool before removing the foil and paper wrapping. This is the best stage for freezing the sausages if you have made a batch. They will keep for up to 2–3 months.

To finish the bean casserole, add the oil, garlic, carrot, celery and shallots to a large, deep pan or wok. Fry gently over a medium heat for 5–10 minutes until the vegetables soften. Try not to colour them. Add the thyme, beans and stock and bring to a simmer. Cook gently for 5–10 minutes and check the seasoning, adding salt and pepper as you like.

Meanwhile, in a large frying pan/skillet, add 2 tablespoons of olive oil and place on a medium-high heat on the hob/stovetop. Add the sausages and fry for 8–10 minutes until browned on all sides, turning as needed.

Add the cavolo nero to the casserole and cook for a further 10 minutes until the cabbage is soft.

To serve, add a ladleful or two of the bean casserole into a large wide bowl and place two sausages on top, spoon over more bean casserole and scatter with the parsley. Serve with crusty bread.

ESCALOPINI PARMIGIANOT
CRISPY 'ESCALOPE' WITH MARINARA-STYLE SAUCE & CASHEW CHEESE

This dish is where vegan comfort food meets that satisfying fast food-style fix. A very cheeky vegan-take on chicken parmigiana with a crispy-coated fillet drenched in a rich tomato sauce and gooey cheesy topping. Satisfyingly rich. Serve with a side of pasta lightly bathed in olive oil; spaghetti or linguine work well.

100 g/2⅓ cups panko breadcrumbs
1 teaspoon dried oregano
75 g/2¾ oz. vegan Parmesan
8 tablespoons aquafaba (see page 12) or use vegan 'egg' substitute such as flax or Orgran
4 mock 'chkn' escalopes (see page 13)
1 onion, halved and peeled
2 garlic cloves
500 ml/generous 2 cups passata/strained tomatoes

FOR THE CASHEW CHEESE
120 g/1 cup cashews, soaked in cold water for 3 hours
300 ml/1¼ cups almond milk
9 g/2 tablespoons tapioca starch
4 tablespoons nutritional yeast
1 teaspoon garlic powder
½–1 teaspoon sea salt, to taste

vegetable oil, for deep frying

MAKES APPROX. 4 ESCALOPES

Put the panko breadcrumbs, dried herbs and half the Parmesan into a bowl and mix well. Put the aquafaba or 'egg' substitute into another shallow, wide dish.

Fill a a deep pan halfway up with oil for frying. Put on a medium-high heat and heat to 180˚C (350˚F). When the oil is hot enough, fry the escalopes in small batches. First, dip into the aquafaba and then dip into the breadcrumb mixture. Ensure each is well coated. Gently put the 'chicken' into the hot oil and fry gently for a couple of minutes on each side, until golden and crispy. Lay on paper towels to drain off the excess oil. Alternatively, to bake in the oven, preheat the oven to 180˚C (350˚F) Gas 4. Spray the mock chicken escalopes with oil and put on a lightly oiled baking sheet. Bake in the preheated oven for 20 minutes until crispy.

In a small pan, place the onion halves into the pan, sliced-side facing down. Smash the garlic cloves with their skin on and drop into the pan.

Put the pan over a medium heat and then pour in the passata/strained tomatoes. Bring to a simmer and simmer for 6–7 minutes with the lid on. Remove from the heat and fish out the onion halves and garlic. Discard.

Preheat the oven to 190˚C (375˚F) Gas 5.

For the cashew cheese, drain the soaked cashew nuts, then add to a blender with all the other ingredients for the cashew cheese. Blitz together to make a smooth paste, then pour into a small saucepan. Heat gently and stir well until the mixture thickens and becomes nice and gooey. Remove from the heat.

In a large, wide baking dish, lay the escalopes into the bottom of the dish. Pour over the tomato sauce and then the cashew cheese on top. Scatter with the remaining Parmesan and serve immediately with pasta and a salad.

KARMA KEEMA COTTAGE PIE
WITH LENTIL MASH

My friend Seema makes the best keema this side of the Pennines, so I got her to help me develop this recipe. I wanted it to carry the full flavours of Seema's keema as much as possible. I love the idea of the fusion cottage pie, because Anglo-Indian food is a large part of our heritage in the UK. In the face of many wrong doings by the British Empire in the Indian subcontinent, as things are now, I do love that my British home feels like a piece of subcontinent India lives here too.

FOR THE FILLING
400 g/14 oz. vegan mince or 250 g/9 oz. dried TVP mince (plus 1 teaspoon Marmite/yeast extract and 2 tablespoons dark soy sauce if using TVP)
2 tablespoons olive or vegetable oil
2 small red onions or banana shallots, finely chopped
3 garlic cloves, peeled and finely chopped
3–4-cm/1¼–1½-inch/ piece of fresh ginger
1–2 fresh green finger chillies/chiles, finely chopped, or use dried chilli flakes/hot red pepper flakes
½ teaspoon ground turmeric
1 teaspoon cumin seeds
1 tablespoon garam masala

1 x 400-g/14-oz. can plum tomatoes
200 ml/generous ¾ cup vegetable stock
1–2 teaspoons sea salt

FOR THE MASH
250 g/1⅓ cups dried red lentils
1 tablespoon olive oil
1 teaspoon sea salt
1 teaspoon ground turmeric
1 teaspoon ground white pepper
1 teaspoon garlic powder
½ teaspoon onion powder

handful of fresh coriander/cilantro leaves, to garnish

SERVES 4–6

If using dried TVP, place in a bowl and cover with boiling water, enough to cover by about 2–3 cm/ ¾–1¼ inches. Mix in the Marmite/yeast extract and soy sauce and stir well. Leave to soak for 20 minutes.

Rinse the lentils several times in a sieve/strainer under a cold tap. Place the drained lentils in a medium saucepan, with enough water to cover them. Place the pan over a medium-high heat and bring the lentils to the boil. Turn down the heat, removing any scum with a large spoon. Simmer for 15–20 minutes until very soft. Stir occasionally and add a little more water if needed, a few tablespoons at a time. You are aiming for no or little excess water. Once the lentils are fully cooked, remove from the heat. Mash the lentils with a fork or potato masher. Add all the remaining mash ingredients and mix well. Return to the heat to evaporate any excess liquid and dry out the mash mixture slightly. Cook over a high heat, stirring well for a few minutes, then set the mash aside.

In a large, heavy-based pan, add the oil, onions or shallots and garlic and put over a medium heat. Fry gently for 8–10 minutes until softened and starting to brown. Add the ginger, chillies/chiles, turmeric and cumin and fry for another few minutes then add the remaining filling ingredients. Bring to a simmer and cook over a low-medium heat for 20–30 minutes. Check the seasoning and add more salt as you prefer.

Preheat the oven to 200°C (400°F) Gas 6. Place the filling in a large oven proof dish. Top with the lentil mash. Bake in the oven for 15–20 minutes until bubbling and crispy topped. Scatter with some fresh coriander/cilantro and serve immediately.

CHEESY CHKN, LEEK & MUSHROOM PIE

This big flaky-topped pie will serve a hungry party of six. I love this pie for many reasons. It's easy to find vegan chicken substitutes at the local shops (or use the recipe for homemade seitan chicken on page 13). And the recipe takes less than 30 minutes to prepare. The unbaked pie also freezes really well for several months, so I often make two at the same time, or several smaller ones to freeze for another time. I don't think anything beats homemade ready-made food!

FOR THE SAUCE
120 g/1 cup cashews, soaked in cold water for 3 hours
500 ml/generous 2 cups almond or soy milk
9 g/1 heaped tablespoon tapioca starch
4 tablespoons nutritional yeast
1 teaspoon garlic powder
½–1 teaspoon sea salt, to taste

FOR THE FILLING
2 tablespoons olive oil
2 shallots, finely chopped
2–3 leeks, thickly sliced
200 g/7 oz. chkn pieces (see page 13) or use ready-made vegan pieces
225 g/8 oz. chestnut mushrooms, cleaned and halved
½ bunch of freshly chopped chives
1 tablespoon Dijon mustard

1 x 500-g/18-oz. packet ready-made vegan puff pastry
plain/all-purpose flour, for dusting
2–3 tablespoons vegan milk, for glazing

SERVES 4–6

Preheat oven to 190°C (375°F) Gas 5.

Drain and rinse the soaked cashew nuts, and add to a blender with all the other ingredients for the sauce. Blitz together to make a smooth paste then pour into a small saucepan. Heat gently over a low heat and stir well until the mixture thickens.

For the filling, add the olive oil to a large deep pan and put over a medium heat. Add the shallots and leeks and cook for 10–12 minutes until soft and translucent. Add the chkn pieces, mushrooms, chives, mustard and cashew sauce. Stir well, then pour into a large baking dish, or several small ones.

Roll out the pastry on a well-floured surface, and put on top of the pie filling. Trim and pinch the edges. Using a pastry brush, dip into the vegan milk and brush the top(s) of the pastry before baking. Make 2 or 3 small holes to allow the steam to escape.

Place on the middle shelf of the preheated oven and bake for 40–50 minutes until the pastry is crispy and golden brown. Serve immediately.

POLISH-STYLE CHARCUTERIE
WITH MAGGIE'S PICKLE THAT GOES WITH EVERYTHING

My Polish friend, Maggie, tells me ham-making is a long-standing tradition in Polish and East European food. When she showed me her old ham press, an inherited Czech artefact, I was eager to try making a vegan version.

FOR THE 'HAM'
2 x 250-g/9-oz. packets of bean curd sheets/skins, dried or fresh
2 litres/2 quarts vegetable stock
¼ teaspoon bicarbonate of/baking soda
1 small leek, washed and thinly sliced
1 teaspoon celery salt
1½ teaspoons ground rainbow pepper
2 teaspoons garlic powder
1 teaspoon onion powder
1 x 200-g/7-oz. packet of firm smoked tofu, cut into 2-cm/¾ inch cubes
1 fresh beetroot/beet, boiled, peeled and diced
1 red (bell) pepper, cored, deseeded and diced
1–2 tablespoons vegetable oil
handful of freshly chopped dill

FOR THE PICKLE
235 ml/1 cup vegetable oil
175 ml/¾ cup Polish pickling vinegar (which has 10% acidity, higher than UK ones)
200 g/1 cup white sugar
2 tablespoons sea salt
2 kg/4½ lb. white cabbage, quartered and finely sliced
1 kg/35 oz. carrots, peeled and coarsely grated
1 kg/35 oz. cucumber, deseeded and thickly grated
500 g/18 oz. onions, peeled and coarsely grated
1 red (bell) pepper, coarsely grated
1 yellow (bell) pepper, coarsely grated
1 orange (bell) pepper, coarsely grated
1 bunch of dill, roughly chopped

MAKES APPROX. 5 LITRES/ 4.4 QUARTS

ham press, ham press 'insert bag' and thermometer (or use greaseproof paper and twine)
sterilized glass jars

SERVES 10–12

To make the 'ham', crumble the bean curd sheets into a large pan and add the stock. Bring to the boil and add the baking soda. Reduce the heat and simmer for 20 minutes. Meanwhile, add the leek to a lightly oiled frying pan/skillet and cook over a medium heat for 10–12 minutes. Once softened but not browned, add salt, pepper, garlic and onion powders. Mix well then set aside. Drain the bean curd sheets. Working in batches, take a large handful, squeeze out the excess water, then finely chop until pulp-like. Place in a large bowl and add the leek mixture. Mix well and, using the end of a rolling pin, pulp until well smashed. Add the smoky tofu cubes to the bowl of bean curd along with the beetroot/beet, (bell) pepper and dill. Mix well.

If using a ham press, place the 'insert bag' in the press and fill with the bean curd mixture. Press down firmly so the press is half-filled. Fold the edges of the bag over the sides of the press, then place the press on top and affix the lid so that mixture is pressed down and is securely closed. Put the press in a large pan of simmering water, so the water covers at least ¾ of the press. Reduce to the lowest heat and cook for 2–3 hours. Use the thermometer to ensure the temperature is 100–150°C/210–300°F. Alternatively, the mixture can be wrapped in greaseproof paper and tied with twine, and then steamed for 3 hours.

To make the pickle, add the oil, vinegar, sugar and salt to a very large pan. Heat gently until the sugar and salt have dissolved, then remove from the heat. Add all the vegetables and, using gloved hands, mix well. Cover and leave to stand overnight.

Bring the pan to the boil while stirring, then remove from the heat immediately and fill the jar. Seal and turn the jar upside-down. Leave to mature for a few days. Once opened, eat within 1 month.

INDEX

A

almonds: watercress ricotta 54
aquafaba 'egg' 12
artichokes: Italian-style bean casserole 131–3
aubergines: masala chickpea scramble 114
Panang curry 37

B

'bacon': bacon-wrapped mushrooms skewers 34
club sandwich 84
coconut bacon 21
mock smoky bacon 12
smoky tempeh bacon 113
bagels: bursting bagel with carrot lox & watercress ricotta 54
bao zi 33
barbecue 'ribs', Korean 107
bean curd 10
Buddha's delight 18
sizzling drumsticks 30
Vietnamese spicy noodle soup 44
Vietnamese vegan 'chicken ham' 14
beans: green jackfruit & 3 bean chilli 126
Italian-style bean casserole 131–3
Mexican chilli sausage sub 88–90
beetroot (beets) ketchup 104
the Berliner 95
'bisque', smoky pepper 74
black beans: mushroom 'steak' & frites 117
boxty Irish pancakes 113
bread: 'fish' finger doorstop butties 66
KFC-style chkn burger 100
lobsta rolls 74
Mexican chilli sausage sub 88–90
sesame toast 70
Buddha's delight 18
'bulgogi', sesame rice balls stuffed with oyster mushroom 26

bun bo hue chay 44
buns, steamed 33
burgers: easiest vegan burger recipe ever 104
KFC-style chkn burger 100
burritos, baby got no beef 87

C

cabbage: Buddha's delight 18
Maggie's pickle 140
'calamari', heart of palm 73
carnitas, jackfruit 103
carrots: carrot lox
cashews: cheesy chkn, leek & mushroom pie 139
crispy 'escalope' with marinara style sauce & cashew cheese 135
nacho cheese 80
Thai fried wide noodles with greens & cashews 25
casserole, Italian-style bean 131–3
cavolo nero, fiery flatbread pizza with blackened spicy sausage, squash purée & 91–3
celebration wellington 121–3
channa dal: seekh kebab in missy roti 96
charcuterie, Polish-style 140
'cheese': cheesy chkn, leek & mushroom pie 139
nacho cheese 80
'chicken'/chkn: cheesy chkn, leek & mushroom pie 139
chkn katsu curry 48
club sandwich 84
crispy 'escalope' with marinara style sauce & cashew cheese 135
easiest vegan burger recipe ever 104
fragrant satay 'chicken' skewers 41–3
giant spring roll stuffed

with mock chicken chow mein 29
KFC-style chkn burger 100
mock chkn/seitan chicken 13
Panang curry 37
sizzling drumsticks 30
sticky seitan chkn hot wings 99
Thai fried wide noodles with greens & cashews 25
'chicken ham': vegan belly bits 38–40
Vietnamese spicy noodle soup 44
Vietnamese vegan 'chicken ham' 14
chickpeas: chickpea chuna quesadillas 77
masala chickpea scramble 114
chillies: ancho chilli & mango dressing 69
green jackfruit & 3 bean chilli 80, 126
Mexican chilli sausage sub 88–90
Panang curry 37
saffron ravioli 61
sizzling drumsticks 30
chimichurri sauce 83
chips 57, 117
chow mein, giant spring roll stuffed with mock chicken 29
chow roll 29
club sandwich 84
coconut bacon 21
cornbread dumplings 126
corned beefy hash 125
cottage pie, karma keema 136
courgettes: shiso courgette scallops 58
cucumber: Maggie's pickle 140
quick pickled cucumber 33
curry: chkn katsu curry 48
masala chickpea scramble 114
Panang curry 37

D

dal, spinach 21
'doner' kebab 95
dumplings, cornbread 126

E

'egg', aquafaba 12
empanadas with chimichurri sauce 83
ex-Benedict 110

F

'fish', faux 52–77
flatbread pizza, fiery 91–3

G

garlic aioli 73
gili gado noodle soup 41–3
gravy, roasted onion 129–30
green rice 87
greens, Thai fried wide noodles with 25

H

'ham': Polish-style charcuterie 140
hash, corned beefy 125
heart of palm: faux fish pie 65
'fish' finger doorstop butties 66
heart of palm 'calamari' 73
lobsta rolls 74
saffron ravioli 61
togarashi tacos 69
hell yeah chilli dog 80
'hollandaise' 110
hotdogs: paprika seitan 'dog' 80

I

ingredients 10
Italian-style bean casserole 131–3

J

jackfruit: baby got no beef burrito 87
green jackfruit & 3 bean chilli 80, 126
jackfruit carnitas 103
steamed buns with barbecued jackfruit 33
jicama slaw 77

K

karma keema cottage pie 136

kebabs (kabob): mock 'doner' kebab 95

seekh kebab in missy roti 96

ketchup, beet 104

KFC-style chkn burger 100

Korean barbecue 'ribs' 107

L

leeks: cheesy chkn, leek & mushroom pie 139

lentils: karma keema cottage pie 136

lobsta rolls 74

lotus root: sea-loving sushi 62

lox: carrot lox 54

tomato lox 62

M

ma po tofu with wild mushrooms 47

Maggie's pickle 140

masala chickpea scramble 114

Mexican chilli sausage sub 88–90

mince: empanadas 83

Italian-style bean casserole 131–3

karma keema cottage pie 136

mock 'doner' kebab 95

seekh kebab in missy roti 96

Thai stuffed 'omelette' 51

toad in the hole 129–30

mushrooms 10

bacon-wrapped mushrooms skewers 34

Buddha's delight 18

celebration wellington 121–3

cheesy chkn, leek & mushroom pie 139

corned beefy hash 125

ma po tofu with wild mushrooms 47

mushroom 'steak' & frites 117

sesame rice balls stuffed with oyster mushroom 'bulgogi' 26

N

nacho cheese 80

noodles: Buddha's delight 18

giant spring roll 29

gili gado noodle soup 41–3

Thai fried wide noodles with greens & cashews 25

Vietnamese spicy noodle soup 44

O

'omelette': ex-Benedict 110

Thai stuffed 'omelette' 51

P

Panang curry 37

pancakes, boxty Irish 113

paprika seitan 'dog' with jackfruit chilli & nacho cheese 80

pasta: saffron ravioli 61

peanut butter: fragrant satay 'chicken' skewers 41–3

peppers (bell): smoky pepper 'bisque' 74

phad see eew jay 25

pickles: Maggie's pickle 140

quick pickled cucumber 33

pies: cheesy chkn, leek & mushroom pie 139

faux fish pie 65

karma keema cottage pie 136

pineapple: sweet & sour mock 'pork' 22

teriyaki pineapple 58

pizza, fiery flatbread 91–3

polenta: cornbread dumplings 126

Polish-style charcuterie 140

pomegranate yogurt sauce 95

'pork', sweet & sour mock 22

potatoes: chips & fries 57, 117

corned beefy hash 125

faux fish pie 65

'prawns' (shrimp): sesame toast 70

Q

quesadillas, chickpea chuna 77

R

raita 96

'ribs', Korean barbecue 107

rice: green rice 87

sea-loving sushi 62

sesame rice balls 26

'ricotta', watercress 54

roti, seekh kebab in missy 96

S

salsa, charred corn 87

sandwiches: club sandwich 84

'fish' finger doorstop butties 66

lobsta rolls 74

Mexican chilli sausage sub 88–90

satay: fragrant satay 'chicken' skewers 41–3

'sausages': fiery flatbread pizza with blackened spicy sausage 91–3

Italian-style bean casserole 131–3

Mexican chilli sausage sub 88–90

toad in the hole 129–30

'scallops', shiso courgette 58

sea-loving sushi 62

seekh kebab in missy roti 96

sesame seeds: sesame rice balls 26

sesame toast 70

shiso courgette scallops 58

skewers: bacon-wrapped mushrooms skewers 34

fragrant satay 'chicken' skewers 41–3

slaws 69, 77, 95

smoky stuffed roast with pinenut, lemon & herb 118–20

soups: Buddha's delight 18

gili gado noodle soup 41–3

smoky pepper 'bisque' 74

Vietnamese spicy noodle soup 44

spinach dal 21

spring rolls, giant 29

squash: fiery flatbread pizza with blackened spicy sausage & squash puree 91–3

steamed buns 33

subs, Mexican chilli sausage 88–90

sumac slaw 95

sushi, sea-loving 62

sweet & sour mock 'pork' 22

sweetcorn: charred corn salsa 87

T

tacos, togarashi 69

tartare sauce 57

tempeh 10

smoky tempeh bacon 113

Thai fried wide noodles with greens & cashews 25

Thai stuffed 'omelette' 51

toad in the hole 129–30

tofu 10

chippy-style tofish 57

ma po tofu with wild mushrooms 47

Polish-style charcuterie 140

Thai fried wide noodles with greens & cashews 25

togarashi tacos 69

tomatoes: crispy 'escalope' with marinara style sauce & cashew cheese 135

mock smoky bacon 12

sea-loving sushi 62

toor dal: spinach dal 21

torta ahogada 88–90

tortillas: baby got no beef burrito 87

chickpea chuna quesadillas 77

jackfruit carnitas 103

V

vegan belly bits 38–40

Vietnamese spicy noodle soup 44

Vietnamese vegan 'chicken ham' 14

W

watercress ricotta 54

Y

yogurt: pomegranate yogurt sauce 95

raita 96

ACKNOWLEDGEMENTS

I am massively indebted to my partner Lee, the love of my life, my unwavering anchor and chief kitchen elf. And my children Roisin and Tevo, who bring joy to our family and are incredibly patient with me when I'm immersed in work.

I'm hugely grateful to our creative team, especially to Clare Winfield and Emily Kydd, who always bring their best creative game. And to Megan Smith and Tony Hutchinson for helping shape another beautiful book. Thanks are due to all the incredible team at RPS, Miriam Catley, Leslie Harrington and Gordana Simakovic. Also to Cindy Richards and Julia Charles for giving me the opportunity to share my lifelong passion for mock meat. I'm finally comfortable with being a very strange vegetarian.

Massive thanks are due to all my friends and colleagues who have supported and had faith in me, and especially those who've helped me push forward with forging new paths when life throws its curve balls. Holly Arnold, Charlotte O'Toole, Seema Gupta, Claire Kelsey, David Fox, Maggie Kowal, Dominic Thompson, Lisa Messina, Andrew Critchett, Anne-Marie and John Goodfellow, Karen Bolan, Debbie Halls-Evans, Ping Coombes and all my MasterChef family, because that's where all this started.